Kerry Kern

Rottweilers

Everything About Purchase,
Care, Nutrition, and Behavior

BARRON'S

2 CONTENTS

BEFORE BUYING
A ROTTWEILER

Purchasing a dog is a commitment that should never be taken lightly. Before you set out to select your Rottie, evaluate your daily lifestyle in terms of how a new dog will affect it.

Is a Rottweiler the Right Breed for You?

Clearly, dog ownership is a long-term commitment. There are a few simple facts to bear in mind when purchasing a Rottweiler: He will need plenty of attention, exercise, and care over the next ten or more years. Every Rottie must be well trained, well fed, and well loved if he is to thrive, and *everyone* in the house must welcome him. Additionally, owning a Rottie is not cheap. Aside from the purchase price, which averages more than $500 for pet-quality Rottweilers, there are basic expenses, such as food, licensing, and veterinary costs. In the case of a Rottweiler, you can expect to spend upward of $1,000 annually on basic care.

Let me be blunt: Owning a Rottweiler is not for everyone. Experienced Rottie owners and breeders will be the first to say that the breed can be "too much dog" for most folks. Owners must be able to properly manage and control this physically powerful breed from day one and provide the lessons and activities needed to keep the dog happy and well mannered throughout his life. A Rottweiler has special traits and requirements that must be considered carefully *before* the dog is brought into your home. Every prospective owner should understand the breed's typical characteristics, needs, and instincts and assess how they will mesh with those of the entire family.

Specific things to consider about an adult Rottweiler include the following:

• **Size:** A Rottweiler is big and bulky, which means he will need a good amount of space in your car and home, and he is affectionate enough to want to always be leaning on your legs when not trying to get into your lap.

• **Temperament:** A Rottweiler is exuberant, which means he may try to jump, especially when young. When excited, he can become the

proverbial "bull in a china shop" and might bump into things and send them flying. A Rottie is smart and can learn a lot, but he can be obstinate and willful, needing a stronger, more willful owner.

• **Discipline:** The need for continuous, dominant leadership is paramount. A Rottweiler is powerful and cannot be adequately controlled by children. When playing, a Rottie can easily knock a child down, and he may become protective of one child playing in a group of children. Adults must *always* monitor this breed around youngsters.

• **Instinct:** A Rottweiler is a dominant breed, one might say *aggressive,* with one sex often not being easily tolerant of dogs of the opposite sex and/or the same sex. It is in the Rottweiler's basic nature to chase and capture, which may make even a normally well-behaved Rottie a potential danger to cats or anything that runs away—including playful children.

• **Hygiene:** A Rottweiler, especially a large male, will drool—especially after drinking or eating. He will also shed regularly, and his coarse hair clings pretty stubbornly to clothing and carpeting.

Fair or not, the Rottweiler is oftentimes thought of as a "dangerous breed," even though the vast majority of Rotties are peaceful, playful, and affectionate. You will be wise to consider purchasing liability insurance to protect against any possible damage done by the dog to others' property or person. Rottweilers look intimidating, which often makes people fearful and quick to sue should anything happen. In some towns, laws have been enacted to ban "vicious" dogs. Be sure to check your town's rulings in regard to owning the breeds they single out for special treatment, as Rottweilers are sometimes on these lists. You will have to be zealous in making sure your Rottie is never allowed to roam free in such a neighborhood, as he will likely be impounded and possibly banned from returning to the home. Fines on owners deemed negligent can be steep, and lawsuits will not only be costly but may end with your pet being targeted for euthanasia.

Without a doubt, Rottweilers also possess many fine qualities, such as loyalty, intelligence, a clownish nature, and a desire to please, but it cannot be stressed enough that ownership of this breed comes with much responsibility. Methods of early and continual socialization and training will be discussed further in coming chapters. A look into the breed's past will also provide some necessary insight into how the Rottie came to be the powerful specimen it is today.

History of the Breed

The modern Rottweiler is believed to have descended from the powerful draft dogs known as "drover's dogs" that were brought to southern Germany nearly 2,000 years ago by the conquering Roman armies. These early mastiff-type dogs were selectively bred for strength and power to haul the supply carts and guard the camp. Over time they interbred with the local herding dogs, and through the generations a new breed evolved.

The breed traces its name to the town of Rottweil, a cultural and trade center that in the twelfth century was a center for the cattle industry and had a high concentration of butchers. Rottweilers were commonly used to drive cattle to and from the markets and to protect the herd and master from poachers. The breed was known locally as Metzgerhunds (butcher dogs), and they were so trusted that the butchers often tied a leather pouch containing their earnings around their Rottie's neck for instant protection from thieves. The early Rottweilers' bravery, courage, and ability to withstand the extremes of winter snow and summer sun made them much revered.

These early Rottweilers flourished until the middle of the nineteenth century, when better roads and transportation methods led to many changes. Driving cattle was becoming outmoded, as the donkey, railroad, and later the truck proved more efficient for delivering livestock to the market. With little work for the dogs to perform, their numbers plummeted. The breed was in danger of extinction, but several German breeders devoted to this tireless worker kept breeding them through the years, striving to preserve the original breed type. At the beginning of the twentieth century, the Rottweiler was discovered to be an exceptional police and army dog, and the breed once again began to increase in numbers.

The Rottweiler breed was first introduced in the United States around 1910 and slowly increased in number until there were enough dogs to be accepted for registration by the American Kennel Club on April 9, 1935. The breed numbers showed a slow, steady increase until the 1970s, when "guard" dogs became the vogue. During the 1980s and 1990s the Rottweiler's

popularity skyrocketed. In 1998 the breed ranked fourth on the American Kennel Club's list of most popular breeds (following only the Labrador Retriever, Golden Retriever, and German Shepherd Dog). In 2008, the Rottie ranked fourteenth on the list, making it the second-most popular breed in the Working Group, behind the Boxer (ranked sixth) and just ahead of the Doberman Pinscher (ranked eighteenth).

Today's Rottweiler

The Rottweiler has been assigned to the Working Group by the American Kennel Club. The modern Rottweiler is a rather large dog, standing from 22 to 27 inches (55.9–68.6 cm) at the shoulder and weighing from 80 to 135 pounds (36.3–61.2 kg). A Rottie is the epitome of great strength—even stronger than his rugged appearance suggests. From his days as a herder, the Rottweiler inherits a protective nature and a tendency to "bump" its charges to get them back into line. His compact musculature gives the

full-grown adult enough power to easily knock a person over. This trait makes the breed a risky choice for families with small children or infirm or elderly adults. Although most typical Rottweilers are gentle and tolerant enough to adapt to the antics of children, breeders suggest that children be *at least* school age before having a Rottweiler as a pet.

Rottweilers possess great intelligence, unmatched loyalty, and a strong guarding instinct. They typically are devoted to their family, and often will bond very closely to one member. They thrive on companionship, so much so that they are prone to following wherever their master moves. Some owners cherish this devotion from their dog; others find it obtrusive at times.

If you are away from the home for long stretches of time and plan on leaving your dog unattended, this is not the breed for you. Similarly, the Rottweiler does not thrive in a kennel situation and should be raised within the household, if at all possible.

Training a Rottweiler

Training is the most important aspect of Rottweiler ownership. A dog of this size and strength *must* be thoroughly obedience trained. A Rottweiler naturally is protective of its owner's property, and if not tempered properly this territoriality can lead to an aggressive nature whenever outsiders are concerned. Although a Rottweiler is not quick to bite, it may see fit to corner whomever he considers an intruder. Basic obedience training should begin as soon as the dog is taken into the home (see "Basic Obedience Commands," pages 62–69), with formal obedience training from an experienced instructor beginning at approximately six months of age and continuing with weekly group lessons until he is at least a year old and performing unfailingly in all situations.

Many Rottweilers exhibit a stubborn streak, making obedience training all the more important. If you are not willing to invest the amount of time needed to fully train your dog in proper behavior, **the Rottweiler is not the breed for you.**

Exercise

A working breed by nature, Rottweilers require some vigorous daily exercise to remain in proper trim. Merely giving them access to a fenced yard is not enough. They need at least one lengthy walk daily. Rottweilers are not well suited to living with a sedentary owner. They should never be tied to an outside leash and left for long periods of time. If this is how you plan on exercising your dog, choose another breed.

Once you have thoughtfully considered these points, and decided that the Rottweiler really is the breed for you, the hunt for your Rottie can begin.

Purchasing Your Rottweiler

At this stage, there are a few additional points to consider:

• **Do I want a puppy?** Although a puppy certainly is adorable, a Rottweiler puppy requires an intensive amount of attention and training. He must be housebroken, and he will need almost constant supervision and guidance over the first six months and training into adulthood. An older dog may be more suitable for some owners. However, older dogs will have had time to establish habits—ones you may not like and may find very difficult to correct!

• **Do I want a male or a female?** A female Rottweiler generally is smaller, calmer, and gentler than a male, and easier to train. All female dogs will come into season twice a year, which can cause some trouble if the dog is not spayed. Males, on the other hand, generally embody more breed instincts and traits: large size, great strength, more aggressiveness, and an overall robust nature.

• **Do I want a pet, a show dog, or an obedience competitor?** How you intend to use your Rottie will affect where you go to find him. If you intend to enter him in any competitions sanctioned by the American Kennel Club, you should begin your search at established Rottweiler kennels, where breeding high-quality dogs is at the heart of the operation. If you want a Rottweiler destined for the show ring, you will first have to do some research into the breed standard to gain an understanding of how a show-quality

Rottweiler differs from the typical specimen of the breed. If you are looking for an obedience competitor, you will want to look for a Rottie from a line that has shown good concentration powers and learning ability. If you are looking for a pet, your selection process will be somewhat less restricted, but it will be just as important.

Sources of Information

The American Kennel Club (AKC) and breed and show clubs are excellent sources for obtaining background information on the breed. The AKC publishes a monthly magazine, *AKC Gazette*, which contains a bimonthly column on each breed as well as general information about training, showing, breeding, and canine health. The AKC also publishes *AKC Family Dog* magazine, which is aimed at the general pet owner. By writing to the AKC, 260 Madison Avenue, New York, New York 10016, *www.akc.org*, you can obtain a list of the current national Rottweiler organizations and the names and addresses of the corresponding secretaries, as well as listings of kennels in your area. The AKC stresses, however, that this breeder information is supplied as a service to interested fanciers and does not imply an endorsement by the organization, which could not possibly evaluate every AKC registered breeder.

The Canine Health Information Center (CHIC, *www.caninehealthinfo.org*) maintains a database of health screening results for individual dog breeds. Sponsored by the Orthopedic Foundation for Animals (OFA) and the AKC Canine Health Foundation, this organization works to identify specific health issues for each breed, supports research into canine disease, aids potential buyers in selecting healthy dogs, and assists breeders in producing healthy dogs. For

Rottweilers, CHIC maintains specific information on dogs with hip dysplasia, elbow dysplasia, eye problems, and heart disease.

Selecting the Right Rottie for You

Typically, when a breed skyrockets in popularity—and demand outpaces supply—there is an inevitable breakdown in the quality of the puppies being produced, as unskilled breeders try their hand at "cashing in" on the boom. Luckily, this has not affected the Rottweiler breed on a large scale. Skilled breeders do more than just produce puppies; they are dedicated to producing puppies that are of conformation quality equal to—and ideally better than—the parents. Breeders work hard to select the best possible breeding partners in the hopes of producing the best possible offspring.

Show or Obedience Competitors

If you are looking for a Rottweiler destined for either show or obedience rings, you will do well to seek out a Rottie that has been bred specifically for this purpose. Many people involved in these sports spend years—often lifetimes—selectively breeding their dogs so that each new generation is as good as or better than the one that preceded it. Top-notch breeders will have had their Rottie parents evaluated and registered with the OFA and/or

CHIC for hip and elbow dysplasia and other possible genetic diseases.

Although a conformation show winner occasionally may emerge from a "backyard" litter, most show dogs trace their roots to generations of carefully bred dogs. Selecting a puppy destined for the show ring is always a risky proposition. Rottweilers are slow to mature, with most coming into full bloom at around two years of age or later. Because most puppies are purchased at eight to twelve weeks of age, selecting a show-quality Rottweiler at this point is a best-guess situation. It is quite common for show dogs to be purchased at a later age, such as six months, when they have

matured a little and the breeder has been able to evaluate their potential more fully. You can expect to pay *at least* $1,000–$2,000 for a show-quality Rottweiler.

Finding a show contender is not easy. Show-oriented breeders often breed on a very limited scale, usually a litter or two a year. You must understand thoroughly the requirements of the breed standard to be able to make any judgment about quality puppies (see pages 45–49). Before you buy, be sure to attend several shows, observe the Rottweiler puppies entered in the puppy classes, and ask as many exhibitors as possible for advice and if anyone has puppies available. An experienced, reputable breeder is

generally the best judge of a puppy's potential, but there is no guarantee that a promising pup will grow into a show dog. To be honest, dedicated breeders rarely sell dogs they think are top contenders to novices. They often keep the best one or two for themselves or place them with experienced owner-handlers. There is a difference between show quality (a potential champion) and "star" quality (a potential best-in-show winner), however, and you should be able to purchase a ring contender if you put some time and effort into your search.

An obedience competitor needs a stable temperament, concentration, a sound physique, and the desire to work (but most important, a good

teacher). These qualities should be found in any well-bred, well-socialized dog. One advantage of buying from a specialized kennel is that the Rottie puppy may have been highly socialized and indoctrinated since birth and encouraged to develop his instincts that would be useful in the sport.

The Companion Rottweiler

When looking for a companion or pet-quality Rottweiler, you have various options. The local kennels in your area that specialize in either show or obedience dogs may have Rottweilers for sale that do not meet the exacting requirements of competition. This does not mean that

they are bad dogs; it just means that they are not expected to be champions because of some minor physical fault (such as a white spot on the chest, light eyes, a long coat, one or more missing teeth). Pet-quality dogs from kennels with good breeding practices are likely to be fine specimens of the breed, with sound temperaments and conformation. An experienced breeder will not have randomly paired any available male and female, but will have selected a specific sire and dam that were well suited for each other and free from hip dysplasia and other inheritable disorders. You can expect to pay $500 or more for a pet-quality Rottweiler.

Remember—not all breeders are working for the betterment of the breed. Be sure to check credentials and stay clear of people who say they specialize in "attack dogs."

Pet Stores and Neighborhood Breeders

With their high popularity, Rottweilers are being bred on a large scale, which means you may be able to obtain one from a pet store.

Should you be thinking of buying a Rottie from a retail outlet, be sure to check into the puppy's beginnings. A reputable shop will carry only healthy, happy puppies. The main drawback to this type of arrangement is that you are unable to see or find out much about either of the parents. Some pet-store dogs are obtained from local breeders, but often they are purchased through brokers who contract with breeders elsewhere. Inquire into how the shop came to purchase the dog and what health guarantees it will supply. You can expect to pay prices at a pet store similar to what you would pay a breeder for pet-quality dogs.

Many pet-quality Rottweilers are obtained from a neighborhood owner who has decided to breed his or her pet. When considering a puppy from such a litter, be sure to check that both parents are registered purebreds and that your puppy is eligible for registration with the AKC. If the owner cannot supply this documentation, then you must decide if this matters to you. The price for such a puppy should reflect the fact that you may not be purchasing a purebred animal.

Keep in mind that breeding high-quality Rottweilers is much more complicated than just allowing two purebreds to mate. With a powerful breed such as this, it is vital that all Rottweiler puppies be produced from parents with stable temperaments and sound conformation. Breed integrity will be maintained only if matings are carefully planned events, using high-quality animals. One plus is that you should be able to spend extended time with the dam and ideally the sire, as well as all Rotties in the litter, before making your choice. You can glean a lot of insight about the care the adults and puppies have received from the owners.

Shelters and Rescue Leagues

Chances are slim that you will find a Rottweiler in a humane society shelter for long, as Rottie breeders, fanciers, and rescue leagues often stay in close contact with shelters and retrieve most purebred Rottweilers when notified that one has been found or abandoned. They then evaluate him for health and temperament, and, if necessary, seek medical care and work with him on needed obedience training. All such Rotties will be spayed or neutered before the dog is placed in a suitable home. Should you locate a Rottweiler at such a facility, be sure to do a thorough check into the reasons why the dog was placed there. There may be temperament problems that are not quickly visible with limited amounts of interaction with the dog, so be sure to take him for a thorough evaluation with your veterinarian before finalizing such an adoption. Additionally, online sites such as *Petfinder.com* provide information on dogs that need homes. Information from animal-care organizations is compiled in a database that is easily searched for available Rottweilers.

What to Look For in a Rottweiler Puppy

When you have narrowed your search and are considering specific litters of puppies, begin your evaluation by taking a good look at the overall environment. The kennel or pet store itself should be a clean, warm place, free from parasites and odor.

• Ideally, you should see the dam (mother) and perhaps even the sire (father) of the litter. This will give you a fairly realistic image of how the puppy will mature regarding size and coloring. Upon approaching her, the dam should

slightly tired, thin, or out of shape. She has just been through a rough few months and her condition likely will reflect that. If you are concerned, you could ask the breeder for a prepregnancy picture of her. If the sire is from the kennel and available for inspection, be sure to see how he interacts with the other animals and people (familiar and strangers). It is vital that both parents be stable emotionally, obedient, and not prone to aggressiveness.

• Inquire why these dogs were chosen for breeding, if they have been mated previously, and if they had been partnered before. If this pairing has produced a previous litter, ask to see any of the resulting puppies or, if they are no longer available, ask for the names and addresses of people who purchased dogs from the last litter. These puppies should be good indicators of how your Rottie puppy will mature.

• The next step is to evaluate the litter as a whole. All the puppies should appear rugged and well nourished. Choosing the best puppy from a poor litter is always a gamble.

The Rottweiler puppy should appear sturdy and big boned, with bright eyes, an alert expression, and a friendly, inquisitive nature. The coat should be glossy and pleasant smelling. A Rottweiler pup should be fairly friendly and inquisitive and should not shy away from humans. Alternatively, he should not appear hyperactive. Watch how the puppy interacts with his littermates, and then remove him to a spot where he is with you alone. This will not intimidate a well-socialized puppy, although he may be a little reserved. He should submit to gentle handling and allow you to physically inspect him.

The Rottweiler matures slowly and an experienced breeder will know best how his or her

never appear hostile or overly shy, as these are signs of an unsteady temperament. Acceptable behavior would be for the dam to act aloof, calm, and stable; she may be curious or friendly toward you, but she should not be penalized for being a bit reserved or standoffish. This is a breed trait. She should be responsive to her owner and should respond to assurances that all is well. Do not be put off if the dam appears

puppies may progress, based on past litters. If conformation quality is important to you, it is vital that you select a breeder with proven credentials and a good reputation.

What Age Is Best?

Most Rottweilers are purchased at approximately eight weeks of age. This is the optimal time for a puppy to be introduced to living solely with humans, as the puppy is developmentally in what is known as the "human socialization period." From approximately eight to twelve weeks of age, the dog forms permanent bonds with those closest to him. If left confined with his dam and littermates at this age, a puppy will bond most closely with other dogs. If brought into a loving home, the Rottie will form a lasting human-dog bond.

It also is essential that a puppy not be removed from his litter during the "canine socialization period" (birth through seven weeks). A puppy's dam plays an important part in the dog's life, as she establishes the first chain of command and teaches her young their first lessons in discipline. If removed too soon from his litter, a puppy will not have learned common behavior patterns and how to properly interact with others of his species. This could result in an adult dog that reacts in an overly aggressive or submissive manner when confronted with another animal. With a naturally

powerful and aggressive dog such as the Rottweiler, it is imperative that the dog be well socialized and able to interact with other animals in a controlled manner.

The greatest advantage to purchasing a puppy (besides being able to play with him during his most adorable stage) is that the owner is able to influence the dog when he is learning how to interact with his environment. The puppy learns a great deal during the first few months of life, and an owner's authority is great at this point. However, a puppy needs an inordinate amount of attention and instruction during those first six months, and an owner must be willing to make this commitment.

When purchasing an older dog, you will be faced with the fact that the dog has already formed a lot of habits, both good and bad.

Although this does not mean that they cannot be changed over time, it does usually mean that indoctrinating the dog to your way of doing things will not be as easy as if you had worked with him from a very young age. However, acquiring a mature dog has some benefits, too. He should already be housebroken, will have had all his necessary shots, and should have gotten through the "wild" puppy days. When considering an older Rottweiler, make sure the dog has been properly socialized and taught to act agreeably around both humans and other animals, and that obedience instruction has begun. As previously mentioned, Rottweilers destined for show competition often are purchased well past eight weeks of age when their conformation can be more properly evaluated. Such dogs should not have been left to the confines of a kennel, however, but should have received ample human attention and socialization during those formative weeks.

The Purchase Agreement

Having selected a Rottweiler, you should finalize the transaction with a formal purchase agreement. This will list in writing all details of the transaction as well as the guarantee that the breeder will supply. The seller must sign the agreement and include the names and addresses of both purchaser and supplier, as well as all pertinent information about the dog: breed, sex, birth date, color, purchase price, and the names of the sire and dam (with their AKC registration numbers, if available).

The types of guarantee will vary from breeder to breeder, but you should be allowed a specified number of days in which to return the dog should he fail a health inspection by your own veterinarian. Work out in advance how this type of situation will be handled: Is the money refunded, or is the Rottie replaced by another (at the breeder's or owner's discretion)?

The breeder should also supply the new owner with the AKC registration application, if you are purchasing a purebred. Most of the required information is to be supplied by the breeder, with the new owner listing the new address for the animal as well as two choices for the dog's official name. It is the new owner's responsibility to complete the form, sign it, and return it with the proper fee to the AKC. If all is in order, the registration certificate should be mailed out in about one month.

You may find that the breeder will have further terms of sale. Many breeders will sell a pet-quality Rottie only on the condition that the new owners agree never to breed him. They often will withhold the dog's registration papers until they receive documentation that the dog has been neutered or spayed. Breeders do this as an attempt to improve the future generations by weeding out from the breeding stock all Rottweilers with obvious physical or temperamental faults.

There often are terms involved when purchasing a show-quality Rottie. The breeder may choose not to totally relinquish control of the dog and may offer him to a purchaser only on a co-ownership basis.

CARING FOR YOUR ROTTWEILER

Proper care of a Rottweiler involves more than feeding, grooming, and housing the dog. Although these basic requirements certainly must be met—now and for the next nine to eleven years—owning a Rottweiler brings with it a greater-than-average amount of responsibility.

An owner must be aware of the Rottweiler's special qualities and must work actively to shape and enhance his natural abilities. This means providing an abundance of affection, exercise, and obedience instruction from the dog's first days in the home and throughout his entire life. A puppy that gets a good start in life has a great chance of growing to his fullest potential as a trusted companion in the home.

The First Day at Home

The first day in a new home need not be overly traumatic if handled properly. It is vital that you supply the Rottie puppy with plenty of love and attention during the first few days. Arrange to bring him home when you have several days free to devote to welcoming him to his new home. If you bring a puppy home one day and then leave him alone the next while you go to work or school, he may feel aban-

doned and subsequently may have a difficult time adjusting. Try to get the puppy in the morning, as this will leave you the entire day to make him feel welcome before he must face his first night away from his dam and littermates.

A Rottweiler puppy is an adorable clown, so it is only natural for you to shower him with love and affection. The more affection and praise you give, the more reassured and comforted the puppy will feel. Speak to the puppy in soft, low tones and treat him gently. You will be a less frightening and more lovable figure if you get down on the floor and play with the puppy on his level. Though hard to resist, rough play is not recommended during the first few days when you are trying to establish a leadership position and the puppy is trying to figure out where he ranks in his new pack.

Show the puppy where his food and water bowls are as soon as you get home, and then take him to the elimination area. It's never too early to

start housebreaking! Finish the tour by showing the dog his sleeping quarters. You can then let him roam about and explore on his own—with you monitoring from close by, of course.

The puppy will soon need food. Ideally the breeder will have given you a few days' worth of the food the puppy has been eating, which you should continue to feed (see page 74 for a discussion of the importance of proper food for fast-growing Rotties). To help avoid a possible case of upset stomach in the already excited dog, cut the normal ration by about one-third. You can resume full rations once he appears to have settled in a bit. Afterward, the puppy may want to explore some more, or he may settle down for a nap.

Until approximately 20 weeks old, a Rott-weiler puppy will need frequent rest periods. He will exhibit great swings in energy levels.

Periods of great activity will be followed closely by periods of sound sleep. The puppy will need his own sleeping area as well as a small bed, sleeping box, or crate (see more on crates in "Crating Your Puppy," page 57). This will form the pup's new "den." Bring the puppy to this area whenever he seems to be tiring.

The First Night

The first few nights away from dam and littermates most likely will be frightening for your puppy. He may whimper or cry and will need some comforting, but do not overdo it. If you bemoan the fate of the "poor little puppy," he may decide from hearing you that there *really is* something to be afraid of. At bedtime you should play with the puppy to wear him out

a bit, but try not to get him overly excited. Bring him to his sleeping area—be it a crate, a penned-off area of a small room, a pet bed, or whatever safe spot you've set up for him. Once he's situated, pet him and talk soothingly to him for a few minutes, and then go about your business.

Although that may sound a bit hardhearted, it is important to establish a routine right from the start and stick to it. This will set the pattern for the nights to come. If you don't want your dog sleeping on your bed or in your room in the future, don't begin that pattern the first few nights. Sharing your bed with a Rottie pup can be great fun, but he will quickly become a 100-pound bed partner if you let him. Consistency is vital, and it helps the dog learn to trust and understand you. Because of this, you can-

not allow the puppy to do something one week that is forbidden the next.

Making the nighttime routine seem matter-of-fact will be more helpful for the puppy than if you draw it out. If the puppy raises a fuss, return after a few minutes and reassure him once more, but *do not linger there or remove the puppy from the sleeping area.* Picking up the puppy will encourage him to continue this behavior, as he will learn that if he howls long enough, you will come and get him.

A puppy usually will fall asleep quickly if you make sure his blanket or bed is soft and warm. For the first few nights, you can imitate his mother's warmth by filling an empty two-liter soft-drink container with hot water, making sure the cap is on tight, and wrapping it inside a thick towel. Many Rottie pups settle quickly

Introducing the Puppy

It is easy for everyone to get caught up in the excitement of having a new puppy in the home, but try not to allow the puppy to get overstimulated. The first few days should be fun but not exhausting. Even your seemingly rough-and-tumble Rottweiler will need to take things slowly. Learning the voice and appearance of the members of the immediate family is the puppy's first chore. Make things easy during the first days by not exposing your Rottweiler to a continuous stream of new faces eager to meet the new puppy.

As a rule, it is easier to integrate a puppy into a household; an adult is slightly less adaptable. Adult Rottweilers usually are least tolerant of other adult dogs of the same sex. Introducing a Rottweiler puppy into a household already containing an adult Rottie often can be difficult, but this can be controlled with obedience training, constant attention, and praise for all the animals. If your dog lives in a one-dog home, it is vital that he be exposed to as many other dogs as possible on a routine basis so that it grows up well socialized. This means frequent trips to "dog-friendly" parks, long walks to meet and greet other leashed dogs, and getting to know the neighborhood animals. Constant praise and instant correction, as needed, will aid in raising an amiable Rottie.

Children

While most Rottweilers are very tolerant and loving toward children, owners must always supervise their dogs when kids are around. No exceptions. Some Rotties do not adapt well to the rough treatment children can inflict. No Rottweiler—young or old, male or female—should *ever* be left alone with an infant. Even

when soft, soothing music is played in the background or you place a wind-up clock in the room. This may relieve the puppy's tension enough to allow him to fall deeply asleep.

Remember to praise the puppy and lavish lots of attention on him first thing each morning to reward his good behavior during the night. Although the first night or two may seem excruciating for all involved, things will quickly settle into a pattern and everyone soon should be sleeping soundly through the night.

a docile Rottweiler is an imposing figure; just being stepped on or bumped by an exuberant Rottie can be dangerous to small children. When there are young children in a household, all meetings with the puppy must be monitored closely. The children must be taught how to gently pet, lift, and handle the puppy. Should the children's high-pitched squeals excite the puppy, he may try to nip at them (as he would a littermate), so be sure to correct him immediately ("*No mouth!*"). Adult Rottweilers will sometimes instinctively bang into children, usually in an effort to move or "herd" them. An adult Rottie can easily knock a child or an elderly person over, possibly into furniture or onto hard surfaces, so it is best to carefully control the dog at such meetings. Because of this, many experienced breeders recommend that Rottweilers not be placed in homes with young children.

Other Pets

Before you introduce the puppy to the other pets already established in the home, try to give the puppy a little time to get his bearings. The other pets surely will sense the new presence, however, so the delay should not be for long. All the pets must be strictly supervised and restrained. Well-trained adult Rottweilers should be expected to react peaceably toward a puppy, but you must be prepared for an unfavorable response by having them on lead. Praise all the dogs throughout the meeting, giving the adult lavish amounts of affection and attention. If any of the animals growl menacingly or lunge at the other, immediately correct with a stern warning (*"Festus, off!"*) and remove the offender from the

room. A new puppy is sometimes thought to be a threat to the household order, and the animals will need to work out a new pecking order, but this competitiveness should ease over time if handled properly. Be sure to give equal amounts of affection to all pets in the home to avoid unnecessary competition. Do not try to always keep the animals apart, as this will enhance any existing tensions between them.

A Rottweiler may exhibit some aggressive behavior toward cats. Because dogs and cats do not understand each other's body language, their reaction when they meet can be unpredictable. A Rottweiler that has been raised with cats generally will be tolerant toward them throughout his life.

Daytime Care

A Rottweiler puppy will need a lot of attention from day one. The impish puppy grows into the powerful adult, and he needs strong guidance and companionship throughout that growing period. Your Rottweiler should not be left alone for great lengths of time, as he undoubtedly will feel abandoned—and most likely will take this frustration out on your house, furniture, or personal property.

Most maladjusted adult dogs began as lonely or poorly treated puppies, and the effects of a poor beginning can be devastating. With a powerful breed such as the Rottweiler, the puppy must be closely monitored and encouraged so that the positive breed traits—loyalty, affection, obedience—become pronounced and the potential negative traits never develop. A well-bred puppy exposed to periods of loneliness and abuse may develop into the high-strung, aggressive Rottweiler characterized in television shows or popular movies as the monster behind the chain-link fence that lunges at all who pass by (see "Separation Anxiety," page 97). Those poor creatures are created by bad owners, and dedicated Rottweiler breeders and owners can wipe out that image by making sure their dogs get a good start by providing them with good leadership, love, and training throughout their entire life.

Every Rottweiler puppy has exercise, elimination, and socialization needs that must be attended to during the day. In today's society, most families have two wage earners and must leave their pet alone. Does this mean that no one who works should own a Rottweiler, or that we are doomed to a generation of neurotic dogs because no one is home during the day to teach them? No, it means that such owners will have to make arrangements for their puppy during the time they will be absent.

As your Rottie matures, he will be able to be alone for longer periods, but while he is young, you may need to hire someone to care for your puppy. In many cities there are professional "dog walkers" or "dog sitters" who are willing to come to your home and care for your pet. Or you may be able to find someone who will watch the puppy in their home during the day to avoid any extended separations. Always make sure that the caretakers are experienced and comfortable with Rottweilers. If you cannot attend to this particular need, do not consider owning a Rottweiler.

If you must leave the home for an extended length of time, try to take your Rottie puppy with you. They are adorable; take advantage of this! If this is not possible, arrange to leave him with someone he is acquainted with.

Puppy Socialization

Socializing your Rottweiler begins while the dog is quite young and continues throughout his life. By frequently handling each puppy and talking softly to him, the breeder has given your Rottweiler puppy his first lessons on how to react toward humans. He should be exposed to as many situations as possible and should regularly meet and interact with other animals and unfamiliar people—with proper responses praised and aggressive or disobedient responses immediately corrected.

Puppy socialization classes, often called Kindergarten Puppy Training (KPT), are informative sessions held by local dog clubs to help introduce both owner and puppy to some basic training and discipline techniques. These classes do not include formal obedience training but instead focus on showing owners some basic handling skills and housebreaking methods. The instructors discuss canine nutrition and health care and provide background information on how a puppy learns and understands.

KPT classes are valuable for new owners of Rottweilers. The sessions attempt to teach various techniques for establishing leadership and gaining control over the puppy right from the start. The emphasis is on effective communication, and the trainers show owners how to behave in a way their puppy will understand. When a dog does not receive the cues he expects from a leader, he does not feel compelled to obey. Puppy socialization classes teach leadership techniques and help produce more effective owners, as well as well-mannered puppies.

KPT classes also are valuable because they expose the Rottie puppy to new people, dogs, and surroundings. They give owners experience at having their dog encounter unfamiliar dogs. This is valuable for Rottweilers, who can develop aggressive tendencies toward other dogs of the same sex if left uncorrected. Owners learn how their dog instinctively reacts in these situations and how to control a negative reaction. Such a lesson can shape the course of how the dog will interact with strange animals when it is an adult.

Puppy socialization classes help the Rottie puppy learn self-control and how to handle new situations. This is confidence building. Such classes can instill a sense of accomplishment and a positive attitude toward training, which is exactly what a leader must instill in a Rottweiler.

Exercise and Housing

The Rottweiler was developed as a working breed, and young pup through adult dog will require some regular vigorous exercise to keep in trim and proper spirit. A Rottie seems to bloom when given a chance to participate in some activity with his master; a bored Rottie may take his excess energy out destructively or overreact to any stimuli he may encounter.

Note: It cannot be said enough that overexercise—just like overfeeding—can have adverse health effects for your Rottie puppy, so be sure to walk and play daily but don't overdo! Should your Rottie puppy exhibit any signs of pain or lameness, consult with your veterinarian as soon as possible. It may be caused by a disorder known as panosteitis, which is common in large breeds and has a good outcome if tended to early (see "If Your Rottweiler Gets Sick," page 83).

Outdoor Accommodations

Although Rottweilers have been kept successfully in large apartments, they do best in homes with access to a large yard. The yard should be fully fenced to a height of 6 feet (1.8 m). Puppies in particular need to get out in the yard each day and work off some of the abundant energy they pack in their powerful frame. A well-exercised puppy is much less likely to involve himself in destructive chewing or digging. Again, monitor him to make sure he doesn't overdo.

Rottweilers usually are content to spend a considerable amount of time outdoors, but they must always be provided with protection from the elements. The breed does better in a cool or temperate zone, rather than in an excessively hot area. Because of their black coat color, Rottweilers are prone to heatstroke if overworked or left outside in the direct sun during hot weather. Be sure to provide water at all times and take it with you on walks. Should your Rottie start panting excessively and showing signs of exhaustion, begin cooling him immediately (see "Heatstroke," page 98).

The Rottweiler that spends considerable time outdoors should be provided with a doghouse to supply adequate shelter against heat, cold, and dampness. It should be large enough to allow the dog to fully stretch out, but not so large that it will not retain heat during cold weather. The entrance should be just large enough to allow the dog to enter easily. A doghouse with a hinged top is easiest to clean.

Place the house in a shaded area during the hot months and in a sunny spot during cold periods. The house should be mounted on platform risers or placed on blocks to stand several inches off the ground, thereby avoiding direct contact with the soil. Do not position the house directly against a fence. Although Rottweilers are not noted climbers, placing a doghouse against a fence gives an excited dog the opportunity to climb up on it and jump the fence.

Traveling with Rottweilers

Most Rottweilers enjoy traveling with their owners, especially if the other choice is staying home alone. In fact, it is terrific socialization for your Rottie to experience as many new situations, sights, and sounds as possible.

Traveling by Car

Begin familiarizing your Rottie with riding in the car from the time he is a puppy. He should always be placed in the backseat. When the car is in motion, it is safest for the puppy to ride in his crate. Many people find this too cumbersome, however, and instead teach their Rottie to lie down during the ride. If your car or van is large enough to have open space at the back, you can purchase a dog grill to partition off an area for him.

To improve air circulation during warm weather, keep the car windows open approximately 2 inches (5.1 cm). Specially designed window screens that allow the window to be opened more widely can be purchased if you travel frequently without air-conditioning during hot weather.

Rottweilers can easily be overcome by the heat, so during hot periods provide the dog with a small amount of water at regular intervals when traveling. Make it a habit to bring an insulated container of cold water with you wherever you go. *Never leave a Rottweiler unattended in a parked car during the heat of the day.* The temperature inside a parked car can soar in just minutes and prove fatal to the dog. Puppies especially are susceptible (see page 98 for instructions on how to deal with heatstroke).

Never allow your Rottweiler to hang his head out the window while the car is in motion. This can result in eye, ear, and throat injuries. Also,

he may lunge against the window in reaction to something it sees, possibly escaping or being injured in the process.

Do not feed your dog for approximately four hours before leaving on a long trip in the car, as a full stomach can often lead to motion sickness. A small amount of water is permissible before the trip.

If your Rottweiler is prone to vomiting in the car and you are planning an extended ride, consult your veterinarian about medication, but

advance. Most hotels and motels will not allow dogs. Travel guides or your local automobile club may be able to supply you with a list of places along your route that will allow animals.

To help reduce the chance of digestive problems during your trip, be sure to bring along an adequate supply of his usual food. Your Rottie already is faced with many new and unusual conditions during a trip by car, so a constant diet becomes an important stabilizing factor.

Traveling by Plane

A Rottie puppy must be at least eight weeks old to fly. There is a chance that at this age he may make the 15- to 20-pound limit imposed by most airlines to travel in a carrier in the cabin as "accompanied baggage," but adult Rottweilers will have to fly cargo. The current domestic rate on the major airlines for a dog and crate weighing more than 100 pounds is $360 and up.

Travel by air has become much safer for animals, but it still can be a harrowing experience for your Rottweiler. Although government regulations have forced the major airlines to better protect the animals in their charge from extremes of temperature and mishandling, the owner should take precautions as well. The first step is to have him checked by a veterinarian to verify that he is in good health. A health certificate issued within two weeks of the trip will be required by most commercial airlines. Bitches in heat or pregnant should not travel by airplane, and any Rottweiler with previous heart or kidney disease should be evaluated by your veterinarian before flying is considered.

• Book your Rottie's flight with *his* convenience—not yours—in mind. Late-night or early-morning flights will ensure that he is not

use it with caution. Most dogs will outgrow a tendency toward motion sickness as they get more accustomed to trips in the car, so medicating your Rottie should eventually be unnecessary. The primary effect of tranquilizers is to make the dog drowsy; they don't minimize the dog's physical discomfort. In fact, tranquilizers inhibit the dog's ability to regulate body temperature, and this could pose problems for Rottweilers, which are already heat-sensitive.

Plan on stopping every two hours on long trips to allow your Rottie to relieve himself, have a drink, and get a little exercise. Always keep your Rottweiler on a leash during such stops, as he may become spooked by the unfamiliar terrain and bolt away or toward something he sees in the distance.

On long trips requiring overnight accommodations, be sure to make arrangements *in*

waiting as cargo on the runway and baking in the midafternoon sun.

• Do your best to get your Rottie on a non-stop or at least direct flight. There is an added risk of the dog being misplaced or injured if he must be moved around to make connecting flights. If your dog must travel on connecting flights, arrange to break up a long trip with a rest stop. Many airports have arrangements with kennels and transport organizations for this purpose. Your dog will benefit greatly from such an arrangement.

• Place the dog in an airline-approved crate for shipping. It should be only large enough for your Rottweiler to stand and turn around in. Dogs that already are accustomed to a crate will be less stressed than first-timers. If possible, allow a newcomer to spend some time daily in the crate for a week or two before taking the actual trip.

• Clearly mark the outside of the crate with "Live Animal," the dog's name, and the name, address, and phone number of both the sender and recipient. Tape another copy of this infor-

mation on the inside of the crate with the dog. If the dog is taking any medication, be sure that it is marked clearly as well. The airline will also apply stickers noting the crate's destination and flight numbers. You will be required to provide written instructions on how to feed and water your Rottweiler over a 24-hour period, regardless of the length of flight.

• Place some soft, absorbent bedding or a blanket at the bottom of the crate for your Rottie's added comfort. Enclose a nylon bone to help alleviate tension and boredom during the trip. Put a plastic water dish near the bars of the windows when he enters the crate, but do not fill it before departure, as this invariably will spill and make the trip uncomfortable for your dog. An attendant will be able to pour water into the crate, should the need arise. A supply of his normal food also should be sent along to help avoid digestive upsets when he arrives at his destination.

• Do not sedate your Rottie before a flight. It is best to teach him to relax in the crate rather than sedate him. Tranquilizers can depress respiration, and this factor—when combined with the possibility of excessive heat and oxygen reduction during flight—can sometimes lead to heatstroke and death. Many airlines will not accept a sedated animal, so be sure to check the airline requirements carefully.

• Lightly feed and water your Rottie approximately four hours before the flight, and be sure that the dog is exercised just before entering the crate. A soiled crate will make the dog very uncomfortable during the flight.

• Check with the airline before departure for instructions on how your dog will be taken on board. Stay with the crate for as long as possible and ask to see the holding area.

• Speak with every airline official you can find who is connected with the flight, telling them that precious cargo is in the crate and where he is going. You often can find the person who is in charge of loading the crate and express your concern about the dog's care. *Hint:* Tip him well and ask him to make sure your Rottie is well cared for and placed on the right plane.

• If you are not flying with your Rottie, be sure you have all his information written down for the person who will be receiving your Rottie, including a tracking number. The crate will eventually be taken to the oversize-baggage area. Unfortunately, animals are usually off-loaded last, so you may have to wait longer than for regular baggage.

• Confirm that the flight has left before you leave the airport. Should there be an extended delay after your dog has been loaded on the plane, ask that the cargo door be opened. If the flight is canceled, you will need to be there to make new arrangements for your dog.

International travel has extra conditions, including quarantine, so be sure to make arrangements for travel abroad—or to Hawaii and the U.S. territories—at least six weeks in advance.

Boarding Your Rottweiler

When you must travel and cannot bring your Rottweiler along, you will need to find good accommodations for him. The best solution is, of course, to have someone the dog already knows take care of him. This should always be an adult that is very comfortable with your Rottie, and vice versa. If this is not possible, make an effort to find a caregiver who is familiar with Rottweilers. A logical place to start is with the dog's breeder, if the breeder is in your area. Many breeders will temporarily board animals. Not only are they familiar with your dog, but who better to trust than someone versed in the particular requirements and traits of Rottweilers?

Many owners prefer to hire a professional "pet sitter" to come into their home several times a day to walk and feed their Rottie. This service is the least disruptive for the pet, as basic routines are uninterrupted and the time apart is less stressful for all. A list of accredited pet sitters can be obtained from Pet Sitters International, at *www.petsit.com*.

Some veterinarians have boarding services, as do commercial kennels. Most of these establishments are well run, clean, and attentive to the dog's basic needs. You can expect to pay from $30 to $50 per day, but facilities differ greatly in the level of attention and space given your dog. Visit and inspect the kennel beforehand and inquire if they have experience with Rottweilers. You want to be sure the runs have ample space and that the staff is trained to handle the breed. Ask about the daily exercise routines and feeding procedures, and check that the boarding kennel is accredited by the Pet Care Services Association (PCSA, formerly known as the American Boarding Kennel Association). A list of approved kennels in your area can be obtained by writing the PCSA at 1702 East Pikes Peak Avenue, Colorado Springs, Colorado 80909.

There are also a growing number of "doggie spas" around the country that offer luxury accommodations, which typically include wading ponds, mist systems to keep the boarders cool when it is hot outside, organized playtime, special diets, Web cams so you can check in on your pet online, and a full grooming treatment before going home. Such facilities are quite pricey, but they specialize in providing your Rottie with a lot of attention and care when you can't.

Whatever the method you use, always leave enough of the dog's normal food to last until you return.

Protecting Your Rottweiler

A sad side effect of popularity has been the number of thefts of Rottweilers in recent years. It may be hard to imagine that a stranger would attempt to steal a Rottweiler from his home or yard, as a Rottweiler's natural protective instincts and loyalty to his home are so well developed that he would usually try to corner any stranger who enters his domain, but it does happen. Some Rottweilers are more affable than others, and professional thieves often employ elaborate methods to restrain or entice a dog to go with them. You can help protect your dog—and your neighborhood—by never leaving him unattended outside the home.

Although many owners think that a tag on the collar listing the dog's name and the owner's phone number will suffice in helping a lost dog find his way home, this protection is limited. The collar could be torn off by the dog or purposely removed by a thief. There are two more reliable sources to identify and find your missing dog: microchip implantation and tattooing.

Microchips

Scanning a microchip has become a widespread method for identifying a lost pet. A tiny microchip the size of a grain of rice is injected just under the skin at the base of the dog's neck. The injection procedure is painless for the animal and the chip is embedded permanently. The microchip contains a registration number that can be read by a hand-held scanner, which is run across the dog's back. Once the chip is read, a call is placed to the central registry that records the specific information on the dog. If your Rottie has any specific medical problems, that information can also be registered and available to whoever finds the lost dog.

Most humane society shelters and veterinarians now have scanners, which are being used to identify a higher percentage of lost animals each year and return them to their owners. The procedure is relatively inexpensive, with many shelters providing the service for as little as $25. Some suppliers include in their initial fee the cost of sending all the information on the animal to the registry, but this may also be left for the owner to do. The cost is generally less than $20 for a lifetime registration.

The two most popular brands of microchips are Home Again and AVID. Owners must remember to send in all necessary papers and to contact the registry whenever the address or ownership of the dog changes. Without current information, the microchip may be useless.

Tattooing

Some owners also opt to have their Rottweiler tattooed. This is a relatively painless procedure that can be performed by most veterinarians for a nominal fee. Many dog clubs also hold annual clinics to perform this service for dog owners. The use of tattoos is endorsed by dog organizations, and show competitors are not penalized for having a tattoo.

The tattoo will be a permanent aid for identifying the dog should he become lost. By law, no

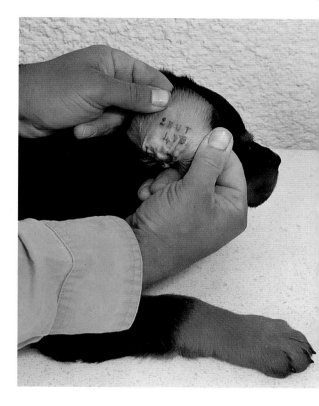

dog with a visible tattoo can ever be sold to research laboratories that sometimes purchase "strays." That alone is worth the price of the procedure. In most cases, your Rottie's AKC registration number or the owner's Social Security number is tattooed onto the dog's left inner thigh. The registration number is preferred over an owner's Social Security number, as the dog may have more than one owner during his lifetime, but any meaningful number can be used for the tattoo, as long as the number is listed with one of the national registries. The largest tattoo registry is the National Dog Registry, at *www.nationaldogregistry.com.*

When you welcome a Rottweiler puppy into your home, you are asking him to adapt to living in your "human pack," which comes complete with a new set of rules and experiences. With plenty of love and attention, your Rottweiler should make the transition from his litter to his new home with ease and emerge in later years as a calm, loving companion. The owner must control the situation from the start and provide the necessary guidance that will produce a loyal, obedient, and properly socialized dog.

Essential Supplies

Prepare for your new puppy's arrival by stocking up on the essentials *before* bringing him home. You will need the following items:

- food and water bowls (select ones that are heavy enough not to slide while the dog is eating or drinking)
- a high-quality puppy food (preferably the brand your puppy has already been eating)
- a crate or some appropriate bedding
- a well-fitting collar
- a training lead

- a bristle brush and hound glove
- a few sturdy chew toys

Puppy Proofing

Your Rottweiler puppy has a curious nature, and he can get himself into plenty of trouble if the house is not "puppy proofed."

- All items that can be chewed or swallowed should be removed, and you should check for any heavy items that are stored low enough to fall on the puppy.
- Be sure all electric cords are secured, as a teething Rottie may try to chew on them.
- Close off all open staircases to ensure that the puppy will not fall down the stairs and injure himself.
- It may sound foolish, but the best way to spot potential dangers is to get down on your hands and knees and inspect each room from the puppy's perspective.

Monitor Your Puppy

During the first few days in a new home, the puppy gets his first lessons on life with the new owner in the new territory. These first impressions can be lasting ones, so make sure these early days are enjoyable and informative for the puppy.

Monitor the puppy's actions and movements at all times. This will keep him from getting overexcited or nervous and will protect him from injury. One of the most common injuries to a puppy occurs when he is allowed to roam and is later stepped on while underfoot. An overly exuberant puppy can jump recklessly from too great a height, and the result can be a broken leg, hip, or shoulder. Constant supervision helps the puppy control himself and helps the owner teach the new houseguest the rules of the home.

Discipline

Discipline must begin as soon as the Rottweiler puppy reaches his new home. The puppy probably has never lived strictly with humans before, so he will have to learn that life in this new pack involves corrections and discipline, as well as lots of love and fun.

Many new owners believe that a puppy cannot learn while young or that trying to get a puppy to obey at an early age will ruin his spirit. Wrong! The puppy's dam already has made it perfectly clear to her pups that there are limits to acceptable behavior and that when rules are broken, there is a correction. The owner must step into this leadership position. Dominance over the dog should be established while he is young, and reinforced daily throughout his life. Some easy ways to exert control are to keep the dog guessing and responding to the owner's wishes. Move his food bowl every once in a while and pick it up momentarily during a meal. When you give it back, praise him for his patience. If he ever gets rowdy, put him on his back and rub his belly

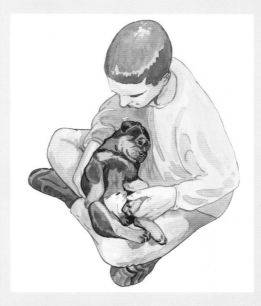

and feet thoroughly. This is fun and establishes control. You may want to change his sleeping place, even if just for a night or two, to prevent him from developing territoriality. Little actions like these mean a lot in imprinting that humans are in control.

The puppy will learn a lot about basic manners during the first days and weeks in his new home. A puppy is a keen observer of body language and will know when his owner is displeased. The trick is to get the puppy to understand what he has done wrong, and then show him the proper action. Corrections at this age should be gentle but firm and almost always can be handled by a quick, verbal scolding. When the puppy corrects his misdeed, shower him with praise. Your Rottweiler soon will be striving instinctively to receive more praise, and this desire will form the basis for all future learning experiences.

UNDERSTANDING YOUR ROTTWEILER

Today's Rottweilers, as well as all modern breeds, trace their roots back many thousands of years to the wolflike dogs that once roamed the earth with the early ancestors of man. One popular theory on how the human-dog bond began posits that the dog initially was drawn to man in search of scraps from the hunt and the warmth of the cooking fire. Humans were, in turn, drawn to the dogs as aids in the hunt and guardians of the community.

Rottweilers are adept at interpreting nonverbal cues. Subtle differences in sounds and movements have significance, and his responses are influenced by the signals he receives.

A Rottweiler will react not only to verbal commands, but also to his owner's vocal tones and physical demeanor. What an owner says often is not reflected in what his or her body language is showing, and the Rottie gets mixed messages. What he is feeling is expressed in his body language, and better communication will result if owners learn the meaning of their dog's various forms of posturing.

Because the Rottweiler's tail normally is docked close to its body, this valuable "mood indicator" is more limited in this breed than with an undocked breed. However, even a stub can give you an idea of how he is feeling.

When relaxed, a Rottweiler's ears are back somewhat, his muscles are at ease, and his weight appears evenly distributed. When happy, his ears are up, and he may whine or give off some short barks. When inviting play he will often drop his front to the ground while keeping his hindquarters up and his tail moving. When alert, a Rottie's ears are pulled forward, there may be some wrinkling on the forehead, the tail is carried slightly above horizontal, his muscles appear rigid, and he is standing up on his toes.

An aggressive Rottweiler will have an angry expression, his flews (the hanging part of his upper lip) will be raised, his ears will be pulled forward, and he may bare his teeth and emit low growls. A fearful dog does not look as menacing as an aggressive dog, but he is unpredictable and therefore quite dangerous. His face is slightly tensed, the ears are pulled against the head, and the overall body position is lowered. If he feels threatened, he can quickly lunge at the perceived attacker from this position.

A timid or submissive Rottweiler assumes a lowered position with ears pulled slightly back, and his fur appears raised. He will avoid eye contact, and his eyes look rolled down and whiter than usual. Humans sometimes misinterpret this as the dog acting "guilty"; he is, in fact, yielding himself to a more dominant authority. A submissive dog also may attempt to lick the mouth or hands of the dominant individual. He may roll onto his back or even urinate. A confused dog also may assume a lowered stance, but he will not grovel or try to lick. Instead, he may pant rapidly, which is indicative of stress.

Communication Tips

Regardless of the impression his size and build may impart to the eye, the Rottweiler is a sensitive dog. The best way to encourage a Rottie to learn and retain information is through positive reinforcement and praise.

Patience, consistency, and praise are a trainer's most valuable tools. To be an effective leader you must clearly show your Rottie what he is expected to do, and praise him highly when the task is accomplished. When mistakes are made, the dog should be corrected promptly and then once again shown the proper action. When the action is finally completed, he should then be praised for his good work.

The well-bred Rottweiler is a capable learner, although some may be more stubborn or easily bored by training procedures than others. Some owners are better trainers than others. Both dog and owner will need to adapt and work out a system that works for them, and this involves trial and error.

When training a Rottweiler, an owner must contend with the dog's pronounced protective instincts. This is a responsibility that cannot be ignored, as the dog instinctively will dislike having strangers approach his owner. Some Rottweilers become agitated every time some-

one comes to visit; the dog may interpret the loud noise and gestures of a friendly greeting as a potential danger to his owner. Your Rottie will need to be taught self-restraint and to accept "outsiders." He may need to be desensitized by constantly practicing proper behavior in such situations. Plan "unexpected" visits by a friendly volunteer; because you are prepared, you will be in a position to immediately praise good behavior and correct overreaction as needed. The way *you* answer the door affects your dog's behavior. Walk calmly to the door; place him in a *sit*. Have your visitor totally ignore your dog. Praise your Rottie and give him a training treat only if he remains sitting. Have your visitor continue to ignore him for a few seconds when inside, and then praise him and allow them to casually meet. Keep it all low-key. If you need help, try to arrange to have a professional trainer come to your house and work with both you and your dog.

In addition, the owner has a responsibility to protect strangers from the dog and never place them in a situation where they are suddenly confronted alone by your 100-pound pet. Although a Rottweiler rarely will bite without provocation, he can easily intimidate the unprepared visitor.

Just as a safety measure, make sure visitors are aware that a Rottweiler is on the property. Post a sign by the front entrance to warn postal workers and delivery people that they should not roam the property alone. Training is the best preventive, but instincts can never be trifled with.

Training and handling the Rottweiler can take skill, and novices should seek out an experienced professional as soon as they encounter problems. In homes where a Rottie is to be primarily a companion, select a trainer who has previously worked with Rottweilers and whose expertise includes more than just the "protection" aspect of this breed. Not all Rottweilers are suited for guard work, and not all owners want to cultivate this side of their pet. Select a trainer who is assertive, but avoid the overly rough one. Every well-bred Rottweiler wants to please his owner, and he does not have to be physically manhandled to be taught obedience (see "Training Your Rottweiler," page 51, for a guide to basic training techniques).

Good communication between a Rottweiler and his owner requires more than a heavy hand; it is a commitment based on sensitivity, patience, praise, and time.

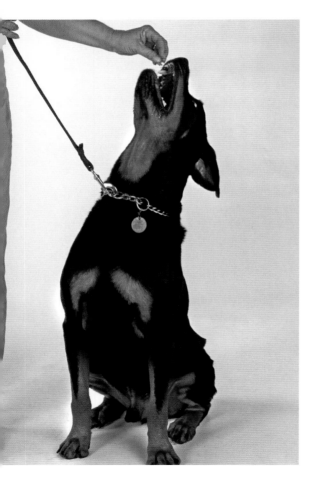

Living with a Rottweiler

No dog owner could ask for a more loyal, loving companion than a Rottweiler. With those he loves, he is openly affectionate and fun loving. With those he doesn't know, he is naturally aloof and wary. A Rottweiler's size and strength make him special, and a special pet requires a special owner. A Rottie owner should be active and include the dog in as many activities as possible. A Rottweiler is not for everyone, but a well-trained and socialized Rottweiler can be a trusted family member and a loving friend.

A Rottweiler requires supervision. His exercise requirements are substantial during the first few years of life but decrease a bit as an adult. A Rottweiler is slow to mature and may not reach full "bloom"—both physically and mentally—until three years of age. His grooming requirements are minimal, although he will shed. His coat is naturally clean and odorless, and his normal life expectancy is nine to eleven years.

A Rottweiler's use as a watchdog is legendary, and this natural guardian instinct ensures that he wishes to remain near his home and loved ones. He seldom will roam.

The Rottweiler is a fearless dog with a high tolerance for pain. An overly aggressive dog could be a danger to all around him, so much care must be taken in the selection and training of a Rottie puppy to ensure that he develops into a calm, controlled adult. Play that is too rough, strenuous tag games, and teasing should always be avoided, as overstimulation can result.

Companionship is vital in a Rottweiler's life. He will not do well without plenty of human attention. When allowed to work with his owner, a Rottie gives wholeheartedly to whatever task he is presented with.

The Working Rottweiler

The Rottweiler breed was brought back from the verge of extinction because of its working ability. Rottweilers have excelled as police and army dogs. Their intelligence and loyalty proved steadfast no matter what the danger or duty. Today, the Rottweiler is the breed of choice for those looking for a guardian, and this attests to the breed's well-rounded personality and trainability.

Show and Conformation Competition

Rottweilers excel in many sports and types of competition. Show-quality Rottweilers are among the most popular entries at conformation shows. For training enthusiasts, Rottweilers take naturally to obedience competition. There are training clubs dedicated strictly to this sport, and obedience trials routinely are held in conjunction with most large AKC conformation shows.

Schutzhund Competition

Schutzhund competition originated in Germany but has become in recent years a major sport among American Rottweiler enthusiasts as well. The training is rigorous. Schutzhund dogs are required to master a combination of advanced obedience, tracking, and protection skills. The training is rigorous. Only dogs with stable temperaments and well-developed protection instincts can excel in this sport, where control and drive are of utmost importance.

The Rottweiler also is becoming a top competitor in weight-pulling competitions. This uses the breed's natural power and strength, and reflects the Rottweiler's heritage as a cart dog. There are several types of competition, including sled or cart pulling, in which the Rottweiler is harnessed and challenged to pull

loads of various weights. Competitors in this sport must be extremely well conditioned, and many began by enthusiastically pulling the children in their household on daily jaunts in the family wagon.

Agility

Agility is a fast-paced sport in which the dog must navigate various types of jumps, tunnels,

and other obstacles. The dog and handler are working against the clock and the times posted by the other exhibitors. Agility originated in England and was brought to this country by the United States Dog Agility Association. The American Kennel Club (AKC) began sponsoring agility trials in 1994. Given the stocky body type of the Rottweiler, the breed is not one of the top competitors in this sport, but many owners find it a wonderful pastime with their pet.

Therapy Work

One of the most fulfilling activities a Rottweiler can engage in is therapy work. Research has proven that animals enrich the lives of humans in ways that can reduce stress and make them happier and healthier. Organizations throughout the world, such as Therapy Dogs International or the Delta Society, have developed programs in which well-trained Rottweilers and other breeds visit the elderly, sick, and even prison inmates. The dogs are therapeutic aids that can help people in many ways—providing help for those struggling to recover from debilitating illnesses, such as a stroke, or as loving enticements for withdrawn and uncommunicative children. This pet-facilitated therapy has proven to be highly successful, and the cost for training is usually just a matter of a few hours' time.

A German-born Rottweiler named Ch. Mirko vom Steinkopf, CDX, was not only an international champion with obedience, tracking, and Schutzhund titles, but also a regular visitor to juvenile cancer patients undergoing treatment at a local hospital. He was renowned for nuzzling the patients and distracting them from their physical problems. Many parents praised this Rottie for helping their children recover from their illness. Such a legacy lives on forever.

The High-Quality Rottweiler

The well-bred Rottweiler is a robust and powerful dog, ranging from approximately 22 to 27 inches (55.9–68.6 cm) in height and 80 to 135 pounds (36.3–61.2 kg) in weight. A Rottie's coat is always a glossy black, marked with a range of shades from tan or light brown to mahogany (with the darker shades more desirable). The markings are located as spots over each eye, on the cheeks and throat, a triangular mark on either side of the breastbone, under the tail, and at the base of the front and rear legs. (Beware of anyone advertising or promoting the sale of "rare, red Rottweilers." A red coat is a genetic fault produced by a recessive gene that inhibits the display of the characteristic black base coat color. Rotties with this trait have a light brown or auburn base coat color with light auburn markings and may have light-colored eyes. They should never be bred, as this fault has been linked to a high incidence of eye and cardiac problems.)

The Rottweiler Standard

The official U.S. breed standard for the Rottweiler, as devised by the American Rottweiler Club (the national breed club) and accepted by the American Kennel Club, is listed below. The standard defines the "ideal" Rottweiler and serves as a guide for judging the Rottweiler in show competition. The details in the standard are goals that dedicated breeders strive to produce in their dogs.

The AKC Standard Rottweiler as approved May 8, 1990; effective June 28, 1990:

General Appearance

The ideal Rottweiler is a medium large, robust, and powerful dog, black with clearly defined rust markings. His compact and substantial build denotes great strength, agility, and endurance. Dogs are characteristically more massive throughout with larger frame and heavier bone than bitches. Bitches are distinctly feminine, but without weakness of substance or structure.

Size, Proportion, and Substance

Dogs—24 to 27 inches [61–68.6 cm]. Bitches—22 to 25 inches [55.9–63.5 cm] with preferred size being midrange of each sex. Correct proportion is of primary importance, as long as size is within the standard's range. The length of body, from prosternum to the rear-most projection of the rump, is slightly longer than the height of the dog at the withers, the most desirable proportion of height to length being 9 to 10. The Rottweiler is neither coarse nor shelly. Depth of chest is approximately 50 percent (50%) of the height of the dog. His bone and muscle mass must be sufficient to balance his frame, giving a compact and very powerful appearance. *Serious Faults*—Lack of proportion, undersized, oversized; reversal of sex characteristics (bitchy dogs, doggy bitches).

Head

Of medium length, broad between the ears; forehead line seen in profile is moderately arched; zygomatic arch and stop well developed with strong, broad upper and lower jaws. The desired ratio of back skull to muzzle is 3 to 2.

Forehead is preferred dry; however, some wrinkling may occur when dog is alert. *Expression* is noble, alert, and self-assured. *Eyes* of medium size, almond shaped with well-fitting lids, moderately deep-set, neither protruding nor receding. The desired color is a uniform dark brown. *Serious Faults*—Yellow (bird of prey) eyes; eyes of different color or size; hairless eye rim. *Disqualification*—Entropion, ectropion. *Ears* of medium size, pendant, triangular in shape; when carried alertly the ears are level with the top of the skull and appear to broaden it. Ears are to be set well apart, hanging forward with the inner edge lying tightly against the head and terminating at approximately mid-cheek. *Serious Faults*—Improper carriage (creased, folded, or held away from cheek/head). *Muzzle*—Bridge is straight, broad at base with slight tapering toward tip. The end of the muzzle is broad with well-developed chin. Nose is broad rather than round and always black. *Lips*—Always black; corners closed; inner mouth pigment is preferred dark. *Serious Fault*—Total lack of mouth pigment (pink mouth). *Bite and Dentition*—Teeth 42 in number (20 upper, 22 lower), strong, correctly placed, meeting in a scissors bite—lower incisors touching inside of upper incisors. *Serious Faults*—Level bite, any missing tooth. *Disqualifications*—Overshot, undershot (when incisors do not touch or mesh); wry mouth; two or more missing teeth.

Neck, Topline, and Body

Neck—Powerful, well muscled, moderately long, slightly arched and without loose skin. *Topline*—The back is firm and level, extending in a straight line from behind the withers to the croup. The back remains horizontal to the ground while the dog is moving and standing.

Body—The chest is roomy, broad, and deep, reaching to elbow, with well-pronounced forechest and well-sprung, oval ribs. Back is straight and strong. Loin is short, deep, and well muscled. Croup is broad, of medium length and only slightly sloping. Underline of a mature Rottweiler has a slight tuck-up. Males must have two normal testicles properly descended into the scrotum. **Disqualifications**—Unilateral cryptorchid or cryptorchid males. **Tail**—Tail docked short, close to body. The set of the tail is more important than length. Properly set, it gives an impression of elongation of topline; carried slightly above horizontal when the dog is excited or moving.

Forequarters

Shoulder blade is long and well laid-back. Upper arm equal in length to shoulder blade, set so elbows are well under body. Distance from withers to elbow and elbow to ground is equal. Legs are strongly developed with straight, heavy bone, not set close together. Pasterns are strong, springy, and almost perpendicular to the

ground. Feet are round, compact with well-arched toes, turning neither in nor out. Pads are thick and hard. Nails short, strong, and black. Dewclaws may be removed.

Hindquarters

Angulation of hindquarters balances that of forequarters. Upper thigh is fairly long, very broad, and well muscled. Stifle joint is well turned. Lower thigh is long, broad, and powerful, with extensive muscling leading into a strong hock joint. Rear pasterns are relatively short in length and nearly perpendicular to the ground. Viewed from the rear, hindlegs are straight, strong, and wide enough apart to fit with a properly built body. Back feet are somewhat longer than front feet, turning neither in nor out, equally compact with well-arched toes. Pads are thick and hard; nails short, strong, and black. Dewclaws must be removed.

Coat

Outer coat is straight, coarse, dense, of medium length and lying flat. Undercoat should be present on neck and thighs, but the amount is influenced by climatic conditions. Undercoat should not show through outer coat. The coat is shortest on head, ears, and legs, longest on breeching. The Rottweiler is to be exhibited in a natural condition with no trimming. *Fault*– Wavy coat. *Serious Faults*–Open, excessively short, or curly coat; total lack of undercoat; any trimming that alters the length of the natural coat. *Disqualification*–Long coat.

Color

Always black with rust to mahogany markings. The demarcation between black and rust is to be clearly defined. The markings should be located as follows: a spot over each eye; on cheeks; as a strip around each side of muzzle, but not on the bridge of the nose; on throat; triangular mark on either side of prosternum; on forelegs from carpus downward to toes; on inside of rear legs showing down the front of the stifle and broadening out to front of rear legs from hock to toes, but not completely eliminating black from back of rear pasterns; under tail; black penciling on toes. The undercoat is gray, tan, or black. Quantity and location of rust markings is important and should not exceed 10 percent of body color. **Serious Faults**—Straw-colored, excessive, insufficient, or sooty markings; rust marking other than described above; white marking any place on dog (a few rust or white hairs do not constitute a marking). **Disqualifications**—Any base color other than black; absence of all markings.

Gait

The Rottweiler is a trotter. His movement should be balanced, harmonious, sure, powerful, and unhindered, with strong forereach and a powerful rear drive. The motion is effortless, efficient, and ground covering. Front and rear legs are thrown neither in nor out, as the imprint of hind feet should touch that of forefeet. In a trot the forequarters and hindquarters are mutually coordinated while the back remains level, firm, and relatively motionless. As speed increases, the legs will converge under body toward a center line.

Temperament

The Rottweiler is basically a calm, confident, and courageous dog with a self-assured aloofness that does not lend itself to immediate and indiscriminate friendships. A Rottweiler is self-confident and responds quietly and with a wait-and-see attitude to influences in his environment. He has an inherent desire to protect home and family, and is an intelligent dog of extreme hardiness and adaptability with a strong willingness to work, making him especially suited as a companion, guardian, and general all-purpose dog.

The behavior of the Rottweiler in the show ring should be controlled, willing, and adaptable, trained to submit to examination of mouth, testicles, and so on. An aloof or reserved dog should not be penalized, as this reflects the accepted character of the breed. An aggressive or belligerent attitude toward other dogs should not be faulted.

A judge shall excuse from the ring any shy Rottweiler. A dog shall be judged fundamentally shy if, refusing to stand for examination, it shrinks away from the judge. A dog that in the opinion of the judge menaces or threatens him or her, or exhibits any sign that it may not be safely approached or examined by the judge in the normal manner, shall be excused from the ring. A dog that in the opinion of the judge attacks any person in the ring shall be disqualified.

Summary

Faults—The foregoing is a description of the ideal Rottweiler. Any structural fault that detracts from the above described working dog must be penalized to the extent of the deviation.

Disqualifications—Entropion, ectropion. Overshot, undershot (when incisors do not touch or mesh); wry mouth; two or more missing teeth. Unilateral cryptorchid or cryptorchid males. Long coat. Any base color other than black; absence of all markings. A dog that in the opinion of the judge attacks any person in the ring.

TRAINING YOUR ROTTWEILER

Rottweilers are the canine embodiment of size and strength. They have excelled in the role of guard and companion, exhibiting superlative natural protective instincts. These noteworthy trademarks of the breed require special handling if we are to produce dogs that are controlled and responsive to the wishes of the owner.

Modern-day dogs retain instincts that can be traced back to their beginnings as pack animals, and this pack instinct affects the training process. The pack contains a hierarchy; the most dominant—or "alpha"—member controls the pack, and the others fall in line behind. The alpha position is one of respect. To obtain control over a pack animal an owner must earn and maintain the alpha position over his or her dog and, in effect, become leader of the pack.

A Rottweiler puppy is exposed to his first doses of discipline shortly after birth. The dam is the indisputable leader of the litter—her pack—and she keeps her young in line. When the puppies assert their independence, the dam reprimands them using growls, a swat of the

paw, or an occasional shake of the neck. These are the actions of a leader, and puppies learn to respect the wishes of the leader and to want to please him or her.

Owners should build on the basic disciplinary framework the dam has constructed and learn to correct and instruct their pets in a way the dogs can understand. Should the dog misbehave, the owner must respond appropriately and consistently.

It is common for inexperienced trainers to react too harshly when training a Rottweiler, because of the breed's size and strength. As with any breed, the Rottweiler responds well to positive training methods. Although a physical correction may sometimes be needed when the dog is being overly stubborn, the Rottweiler does not need rough treatment to make him respond.

A good owner corrects firmly but fairly every time the dog misbehaves, letting him know what behavior is correct and what will not be tolerated. The Rottweiler is an intelligent, sensitive animal that wants to please his owner. Although a dog undoubtedly will test his owner's authority from time to time, there is no need to crush his spirit through rough handling and physical abuse. Correct him in a manner he will understand—a firm vocal reprimand, a stern look, or even a guttural growl. He should already understand the method and the meaning. Be sure never to whine, nag, plead, or preach at your Rottie, as these are not the actions of a leader. Rottweilers respond best to training methods taught with consistency, clarity, and patience.

Obedience is based on respect. If your Rottweiler does not respect you, he will not obey (unless out of fear—the worst possible case for a breed such as a Rottweiler, because a fearful dog is unpredictable). To earn the dog's respect, the owner uses abundant praise in response to good actions and clear corrections in response to misdeeds.

Rules for the Trainer

Lessons in basic house manners can begin from the time your Rottweiler first enters the home. Habits learned during the first days in the home are deeply ingrained, so be sure to monitor the puppy's actions. Your puppy thrives on attention, so ignoring him when he does something inappropriate and making him feel like a genius when he does something right is often the best way to get him to feel properly

TIP

Giving Commands

- Your tone of voice is very important when issuing commands. The command should be firm and authoritative.
- Keep things simple. Many trainers include the dog's name in all commands requiring motion (*come* or *heel*) but omit it from corrections or commands that require the dog to remain motionless (*sit, stay,* or *down*).
- Use the *same command* each time you request a certain action (not *"Festus, come"* one time and *"Come here, boy"* the next). Some dogs may react to *"Enough!"* or *"Thank you!"* better than "*No*" or "*Good boy!*" Once you've decided what works best for you and your dog, stick with it. Consistency and clarity are the most important factors.
- The word "*no*" is used so much that some dogs become immune to hearing it, so many trainers use *"Wrong!"* in reaction to a failure to comply with a command and a two-word reprimand—*"No jump!"* or "*No chew!*"—when he is about to misbehave or is caught in the act. Immediately correct each improper response, repeat the command, show the dog the proper response, and lavish with praise when he is successful.
- Try to keep your talking to a minimum. Use simple, clear commands and repeat them only when necessary. Your goal is to have your Rottie respond correctly in response to one command. If he needs constant prompting, he is not responding correctly and probably is confused about what you want him to do.

motivated. Gently but firmly correct misdeeds that you can't ignore with a firm *"Festus, no!"* to show him what is unacceptable, but don't forget to enthusiastically praise him when he does things right.

Getting a puppy to respond to his name is an important early lesson. This is accomplished easily by simply using the dog's name whenever you want him to come and lavishly praising him when he responds. He will love the attention he is getting and subconsciously will learn how you look and react (verbally and nonverbally) when you, too, are pleased. This is the puppy's first success, and he discovers that a correct response brings rewards. Positive reinforcement is the most effective method for making a puppy want to please you, and it paves the way for a positive attitude about training.

Initial Lessons

Most Rottweilers can begin learning the basic obedience commands at approximately six to eight months of age. Concentration is the key. If the puppy wanders off—either physically or mentally—he probably is too young for formal training lessons.

The initial lessons should be limited to no more than ten minutes, but they should be held two or three times each day. Repeat each lesson frequently, but stop as soon as he loses interest. Boredom can seriously damage a training program, and a bored Rottweiler often will react by stubbornly refusing to obey.

The atmosphere should be pleasant, but serious. To encourage the dog to perform well for you, praise each minor success with *"Good, Festus!"* or *"Good boy!"* and some pats. Don't get overly exuberant, however, or he will get so excited that he forgets what he is supposed to be doing.

Corrections

Corrections are an important part of the learning process. The trainer must correct swiftly, fairly, and consistently. Patience is essential, and the correction should not be made out of anger. In most instances, your Rottweiler is confused about what you want and is not misbehaving willfully. Shouting at or striking him will only make matters worse. This is a common mistake with Rottweilers, as uninformed people think a dog of this size needs extraordinary amounts of restraint and punishment. In reality, proper guidance and praise will encourage a Rottie to do well and will make him more responsive to the will of the owner. Few Rottweilers are bullied easily into submission by physical abuse. Such a dog will never be reliable, because he will respond to commands simply to avoid more punishment.

Keep the lessons short and pleasant so that your dog will remain eager to learn. End each lesson with lots of praise and petting, and follow this with a pleasant activity, such as a walk or favorite game. This special attention lets him know you are pleased with his performance. With such positive reinforcement, your Rottie will learn to enjoy training rather than dread it.

Housebreaking

Housebreaking a Rottweiler puppy can be accomplished quickly if the owner keeps close tabs on the puppy during the first few weeks in the home. The most important thing to know is *when* a puppy will need to eliminate: after eating, after waking, after strenuous play, the first thing in the morning, and the last thing at night. The puppy should always be taken to his designated toileting area at these times. Because a puppy has very limited capacity, he will need to go at other times as well, and he usually will give some physical clues that he needs to eliminate: He looks uneasy, sniffs the ground, and walks in circles, as if searching for something.

Housebreaking also is aided by the fact that dogs have an instinctual desire to keep their "den" area clean. This instinct already has been ingrained in the puppy by his mother. When the litter is young, the dam cleans up each puppy's eliminations by ingesting them. When the pups are no longer newborn, she will no longer tolerate their eliminating near the sleeping area. When the puppies soil the den, she corrects them and they soon learn to do it elsewhere. When a puppy is raised by its dam until

CHECKLIST

Avoiding Accidents

The elapsed time between a successful trip to the elimination site and "an accident" is short, so the owner must be alert. Quick housebreaking depends in large part on the owner's attentiveness:

1. Monitoring and understanding a puppy's physical signs of impending elimination;
2. Getting him to the proper elimination area in time, and praising every success.

weaned, he usually knows that some areas are acceptable for elimination and others are not. The new owner needs to build on this.

Accidents

Until a puppy is at least four to six months of age, he has limited control and cannot "hold it" for long. "Accidents" are inevitable, and the puppy should not be punished or hit. Above all, *never rub the puppy's nose in urine or excrement.* Such acts will do nothing but confuse the dog and make matters worse. The owner should show displeasure by pointing at the spot and saying, *"Festus, no!"* in a stern tone of voice. The owner must then give the puppy a clear indication of what *proper* procedure is by taking him to the elimination area and praising.

What do you do when you discover that an "accident" has occurred while you were not with your Rottie? It is a common misconcep-

tion that a dog that skulks away from an owner who has discovered an unwanted deposit is feeling the pangs of a guilty conscience. In reality, he is exhibiting the typical signs of fear and confusion. He is running for cover, not feeling ashamed.

Dog trainers disagree on whether or not you can correct and discipline a dog for an act that you did not witness firsthand, but I believe that you can show a dog what displeases you if you make a connection in the dog's mind between the evidence and your surly reaction to it. Do not overreact when you find an unwanted deposit. You want to let the dog know you are displeased, but you need to show him exactly what you are displeased about.

1. To make a connection in the dog's mind with your displeasure and the waste, bring the dog to the spot.

2. Point at the excrement and scold in a low, guttural tone.

3. Immediately bring the dog to the proper elimination area. Praise him if he goes there.

4. When you both return to the house, banish him to his sleeping quarters for a short "time-out" and then clean up the mess. Case closed.

By making the dog connect your displeasure directly with the excrement and the banishment, your Rottie has been shown that this act will not be tolerated—even when the owner is not present.

Tips for Housebreaking Rottweiler Puppies

During waking hours a young puppy should be taken out almost hourly to be given a chance to eliminate. You will not have to keep this up throughout his life, as he soon will get better control of his bodily functions, but paying a lot of attention to this task really is worth the effort. The number of required walks will gradually diminish to three a day when the dog reaches maturity. Don't rush the pace, however,

because the pressured and punished puppy can wind up as a chronic soiler when mature.

Always accompany your puppy outside when it is time for elimination. You cannot just open the door, let him out, and expect him to eliminate. A puppy is distracted easily and most likely will spend his time outside playing. Later, he will relieve himself inside, much to the despair of the owner who "just took him out." During the training period the owner needs to instruct the puppy on where to go, and most of all, the owner must be present to lavish the puppy with praise when he succeeds.

Until the puppy is reliably housebroken, his movements must be restricted. Instinctively a puppy does not want to soil his den, but he does not regard other places as highly. When not under direct supervision, the unhousebroken dog should be confined to either the sleeping area or the elimination area.

Select a small, uncarpeted, "puppy-proof" area for the initial sleeping area, and make sure that all escape routes are blocked off. A mesh baby gate will do well while the Rottweiler is small, but it may not be high enough or sturdy enough when he has grown a bit. The elimination area should be outside, rather than a papered area in the house, if possible. Paper training is necessary only when an owner cannot be present in the home for long stretches of time during the training process. Crating is also a very effective method for housebreaking (see "Crating Your Puppy," below).

Immediately take the puppy to the elimination area whenever he shows signs of needing to go. Praise each success. When mistakes are made, show your displeasure so that the dog makes a connection with your mood and the "accident," and then immediately take him to the correct spot.

By removing the puppy's water bowl at night and feeding only the prescribed amount of food (no snacks) on a regular schedule, the owner can help to regulate the puppy's elimination needs.

Crating Your Puppy

Dog crates are effective training tools and should not be regarded as cages or prisons. Dogs, as pack animals, will instinctively seek out the confinement and security of a den. When used properly, a crate becomes the dog's den, and most dogs regard it as a peaceful place to rest and relax. A Rottweiler will almost always sleep the majority of time he is in his crate. Most dogs adapt quickly to a crate and will instinctively try to keep this area clean by not eliminating in it. When paired with a regular schedule of walks and feedings, a crate can greatly aid the housebreaking task.

The crate must be large enough for your Rottweiler puppy to comfortably sit or lie down in, but not so large that it gives him enough room to subdivide the space into a bed area and an elimination area. The bottom of the crate can be lined with a blanket for some additional comfort, or you can purchase a crate cushion from a pet store.

When devising a housebreaking program, put the puppy on a regular schedule. A growing Rottweiler puppy must be fed at least three times a day and must be taken out frequently to be given a chance to eliminate. The crate can be used for brief periods between the walks, and as the dog matures, the crating time can increase. A puppy has a very limited capacity to "hold it" and will be forced to relieve himself in the crate if confined for too long a time. This defeats the major benefit of a crate—to create

an area for the dog in which he will not want to eliminate.

The owner must take the dog to his proper elimination area at regular intervals and enthusiastically praise him every time he relieves himself there. During the first few cratings the owner may want to remain in the same room with the puppy to help him feel at ease, but the owner should pay no attention to the puppy. If he senses anxiety or guilt in his owner's behavior, he may well act up to gain the owner's attention, or he may decide that the crate really is something to be afraid of because his owner obviously is upset by it.

During housebreaking start by crating the puppy for only 10 to 15 minutes at a time, gradually increasing the duration over the next few weeks. Physical needs vary from dog to dog, so the following schedule should be adapted as necessary to your particular Rottweiler: During the day, puppies under 12 weeks of age may remain in the crate for up to one hour; puppies 12 to 16 weeks of age may be crated for up to two hours; older puppies may stay a maximum of three to four hours; and all ages can be crated overnight.

The location of the crate is important. Place it out of the direct line of household traffic but not somewhere that will make the dog feel isolated. You can give him an unbreakable nylon bone to help relieve any boredom, but don't give him small chew toys, which can be easily torn into chunks by an excited Rottweiler and possibly choked on. Bowls of food or water do not belong in the crate during the housebreaking process.

Once the dog is fully housebroken, many owners think the crate is no longer needed. However, many dogs appreciate having such a den and will continue to return to their open crate for naps.

Paper Training

Because most Rottweilers will not gain enough bladder control to last through the day until approximately six to twelve months of age, papers or "training pads" probably will be required during this time unless access to the outdoors is provided. Outdoor training still should be encouraged, and working owners should walk their puppy just before leaving each morning and as soon as they arrive home. A brief walk at midday, if possible, is helpful.

An unhousebroken puppy should always be confined whenever he cannot be supervised directly. Provide him with only enough space to have three separate areas: an elimination area, a feeding area, and a crate or sleeping area. If given too much room, he will not feel compelled to use your selected elimination spot. Cover the elimination area with several layers of newspapers or a training pad, making sure not to allow this to extend into the other two areas. Although training pads cost more than newspapers, most have a liner that prevents urine from leaking through to the floor, and many are treated with deodorizers and scents to actually attract the puppy. Some are even reusable.

Whenever you think the puppy needs to eliminate, and every time he seems agitated, place him on the papers. Stay with the puppy and encourage him with *"Do your business, Festus"* or any similar phrase that does not include the terms *come, sit,* or *down,* which will be used later as basic obedience commands.

Praise him enthusiastically whenever he uses the papers. He should learn quickly that this spot is acceptable for elimination—and that you are pleased when he goes there.

To help your dog find his way back to the elimination site, place a small piece of previously soiled paper on each new stack of newspapers whenever you change them.

A paper-trained Rottweiler will adapt to using the outside when he is mature enough to wait for access and when shown that he is supposed to use a new elimination spot. Shrink the size of the newspaper pile until it is small and then remove it entirely. You can help the transition by placing a small soiled patch of papers outside a few times to familiarize the dog with the new elimination spot.

Cleaning Up Waste

In many cities, owners who do not clean up after their pets can be fined from $50 to $500. Cleaning up dog waste not only rids the streets and public areas of repugnant and potentially harmful materials, but also proves that dog owners have good manners.

"Pooper-scoopers" designed for picking up waste can be purchased from pet stores, or the task can be accomplished easily—and sanitarily—using just an inverted plastic bag.

Collars and Leads

There are many styles of collar available for your Rottweiler, including those that snap, buckle, choke, pinch, and "gently lead." You will need several during the first two years as your Rottie grows. You need to buy one that fits, not one your Rottie will eventually grow into. The proper fit for all but the choke collar is one that is snug enough that he can't get it off, but loose enough for you to fit two fingers comfortably under it.

Choke Collar

A training choke or "slip" collar is a training tool that allows you to correct your Rottie with a quick popping movement. It has a ring on each end and is generally made of chain metal links, although nylon versions are also popular. When pulled upward, the collar momentarily tightens around the dog's neck. Once the pressure is released, the collar immediately loosens. The Rottie will quickly learn that an upward tug indicates displeasure and that a correction is needed. The choke collar should be worn only during teaching sessions, and it should never be used to inflict pain.

A correctly fitting choke collar measures approximately 2 inches (5.1 cm) more than the diameter of the dog's head. Because this collar is designed to provide quick, snap-tight corrections, it is pointless to buy an oversized collar because it will not close quickly and can, in fact, be dangerous if allowed to hang loose. *To form the choke collar*, slip the chain through one of the rings. The lead attaches to the free ring. The side of the chain connecting to the free ring must be placed over the top of the neck, not under. In this position the collar will release instantly whenever the upward pressure is released.

Lightweight Collars and Tags

If you want your Rottweiler to wear identification, select a lightweight collar that can be left on at all times. Attach a small metal medallion listing the dog and owner's names, address, and phone number. If he has any health problems, such as diabetes, you may want to purchase a special medical tag and attach that as well. (See "Microchips," page 34, for more methods for identifying a lost pet and registering medical problems.)

Harness

A dog harness is designed to distribute pressure across your dog's torso rather than strictly on his neck when on lead. Although this can be useful when walking a mature, fully trained Rottie, it is not recommended during training. A harness actually allows a dog to pull more effectively and comfortably!

Gentle Collars and Prong Collars

The gentle collar has a loop that encircles the dog's muzzle and a strap securing it around the neck. The leash attaches under the chin. It is often recommended for dogs that pull against their collar or harness. The premise behind the design is that when you control a dog's head, you control his body as well, and that this is similar to the way a mother dog corrects her young.

A prong or "pinch" collar is a chain of interlocking steel links containing two prongs that sit against the dog's neck. When "popped" for a correction, the prongs pinch the skin in a narrow band around the neck and immediately release. It can be an effective tool for those Rottweilers that are not highly touch sensitive. A Rottie's neck is quite muscular, and the quick pop of a normal choke collar may not make an immediate impression.

Many Rotties do not like the gentle leader, and many people think the prong collar is cruel. Frankly, no collar can be expected to correct improper training, which is an absolute necessity for Rottweilers. If you are using either of these collars because training isn't going well, you need to consult with a professional trainer for further instruction. Corny as it sounds, you need to be the gentle—but dominant—leader!

Shock Collars

Sometimes known as "remote training collars" or "electronic collars," a shock collar contains two metal probes that make contact with a dog's neck and administer an electric shock of varying intensity when the owner presses a remote control. Having to resort to such a device is evidence that something is fundamentally wrong with the Rottie's training. Seek professional help and/or reevaluate whether you should even own a Rottweiler.

Muzzles

Despite the fact that the vast majority of Rottweilers are good canine citizens, some towns (especially in Europe) now require that certain dog breeds—sometimes including the Rottweiler—must wear a muzzle when in public or the owner will be subject to a fine. In addition, some groomers and veterinarians prefer to work on your dog while he is wearing a muzzle.

You must select one that fits properly and comfortably. This requires making several measurements of the nose, head, and neck. A leather muzzle is light enough for regular use, but a wire basket muzzle may hold up longer. If you are going with a wire basket muzzle, select one with padding on the snout. A light mesh muzzle can be also be used, but a Rottie may be able to break this if he struggles to get it off.

Another possible use for a muzzle is to discourage your Rottie from injuring himself by chewing or excessively licking his skin in reaction to some health problem. This is a temporary means of aiding a medical solution.

If you are considering buying a muzzle for your Rottweiler for any other reason, you are probably having aggression problems with your dog. That is another big red flag that professional help is needed for both you and your Rottie.

Training Leads

Training leads are made of nylon, woven cloth, or leather and come in various lengths and widths. Most trainers suggest a sturdy 6-foot (1.8-m) lead, $1/2$ to 1 inch (1.3–2.5 cm) in width, although a 3-foot (91-cm) lead sometimes is used when more control is necessary, and a longer line will be needed for teaching recalls.

Never allow the dog to chew the lead. Correct with a firm *"No chew!"* and give the lead a light upward tug to remove it from the dog's mouth. Many puppies are taken aback by the feel of this new weight around their neck, so you may want to let the puppy drag the lead behind him for a while. Remain close by to make sure the puppy does not get tangled up in the lead and get hurt.

When your Rottie puppy seems comfortable with the lead, pick it up but apply no direct pressure on the dog's collar. Follow the puppy wherever he goes for a few minutes, and then let him know it is time to reverse the pattern. Introduce the feel of a light upward tug whenever the puppy pulls on the lead. The puppy may be stunned by this intrusion, or even annoyed. Verbally reassure him in a calm, natural tone of voice that there is nothing to be afraid of (but do not pet him), and continue to apply the pressure when the puppy wanders out of your con-

trol area. The puppy should learn quickly that his actions are indeed under restraint and that the tugs require a corrective action.

Basic Obedience Commands

From the earliest days in the home, owners must establish control over their Rottweiler by monitoring his actions and correcting all misdeeds in a way that makes it clear to the dog what is not acceptable and what the correct course of action is. The Rottweiler is not the right breed for the timid, uninterested, or absent owner. Every Rottweiler will require careful supervision and dominance training throughout his life.

Rottweilers have a tendency to be stubborn, but they can be capable learners if the owner knows how to get the dog's attention and interest. Patience is a must! Formal obedience training from a trainer experienced with this breed is recommended for all but seasoned owners, generally from 6 to at least 12 months. The trainer should be effective, but he or she should not be overly rough with the dog. Some trainers tend to be rougher with Rottweilers than necessary, based solely on reputation. A good trainer should evaluate each dog and base the lessons on that particular animal. Some of the most influential trainers base their methods on positive experiences for the dog, not on harsh disciplinary techniques. Inexperienced trainers often punish a Rottweiler's mistakes too severely, basing their treatment on the dog's size, strength, and reputation. A good handler can control and train his or her dog through a combination of verbal reprimands, physical corrections, and effective instruction, but this takes experience with the breed.

Owners of Rottweilers cannot consider their dogs trained until they obey instantly, given only one command. This cannot be a hit-or-miss situation, where he obeys *most* of the time. A Rottweiler must be reliable *every time* he is called on to obey your command. Accept no less, because a Rottweiler will try to get away with a less-than-perfect performance once you begin to permit it.

Every Rottweiler must learn at least the five basic commands: *sit, stay, heel, come,* and *down.* I consider these the necessary manners a dog must have if he is to live well among humans. The following descriptions of the basic obedience exercises will aid in your instruction. They serve only as outlines, because there are as many methods used in practice as there are trainers. Because every dog responds differently, your task is to find the method that works best for you and your particular dog.

To enhance the dog's concentration, begin by practicing only indoors in a quiet area free from distractions. The dog should be on lead for all the basic exercises. Rottweilers instinctively do not like to look directly at anyone, so you must work hard to get and retain the dog's attention throughout training lessons. Many Rottweilers also have a high resistance to pain and are unfazed by the corrective snap of the choke collar. I've had good results by adding a startling sound in addition to the corrective neck jerk, which is accomplished by just slapping my own thigh to make a popping sound.

Sit

The formal *sit* calls for the dog to sit at your left side, with his shoulders square to your knee.

1. Position your Rottie on your left side, and hold the bulk of the lead in your right hand.

Keep the lead taut and apply some upward pressure to help keep his head up. If he is responsive to your motions, you can lead him into the *sit* by raising your left hand over his head and moving your hand back toward his rear as you command *"Sit."* If he follows your motion, he naturally will fall back into a *sit*; more often you will have to help him with slight pressure.

2. Place your left hand on his rear as you command him to *"Sit"* and press down until he is in the sitting position. (Note that some trainers discourage pressing down, particularly in dogs that are prone to hip dysplasia.) When your Rottie moves out of position, use your left hand to straighten him; your right hand continues to supply the moderate upward pressure from the lead.

3. Praise him highly and give him a few pats when he is positioned properly. It is important to praise when he *reaches* the *sit* position, not when he gets up, because he must learn to associate your praise with the sitting action.

4. Release with *"Good boy!"* and/or an upward sweep of your left hand (the sweep is used in later, more advanced exercises).

During the first few lessons keep the *sits* quite short. In this way your Rottie has little chance to fall out of the proper position or lie down. Gradually increase the time he is to sit. Whenever he moves out of position, correct with *"No, Festus!"* and a light jerk from the lead, and then immediately put him back in place.

Rottweilers take quickly to this command, and you should not need to press on the rear long before the sitting action becomes habitual in response to the command. Once your Rottie is performing the *sit* reliably, you can move on to the *stay* and *heel* commands, which build on this.

Stay

It is foolish to rush ahead and begin work on the *stay* if your Rottie is not performing the *sit* reliably. In all training, **slower is better**.

1. Begin training the *stay* by placing your Rottie in a *sit*, keeping some upward pressure on his neck from the lead in your right hand.

2. As you command *"Stay!"* simultaneously take one step away from him, using your right leg (which is the farthest from the dog) to step off.

3. Bring the palm of your left hand down toward his face, stopping just short of his muzzle, in time with the command and the step.

4. Retain eye contact, if possible (since many Rottweilers feel threatened by constant eye contact, do not insist on a stare-down between you and the dog).

5. As soon as you anticipate movement by your Rottie, repeat the command while maintaining the signal.

He undoubtedly will try to move toward you once he sees you move away, or he will try to lie down. When your Rottie breaks the *stay*, return him immediately to the *sit* and repeat the whole procedure. Ten seconds is enough time for the first *stay* attempts, so release him quickly and praise.

The *stay* involves a lot of self-restraint on the dog's part, so be patient and do not expect immediate results. Correct each infraction and try again, but do not bore your Rottie with endless repetitions. The *stay* should not be practiced continuously. Spring it on him every now and then, and praise each little success lavishly.

As your Rottie shows signs of understanding the *stay* command, slowly extend the length of the *stay* and the distance you move away from him. Once he thoroughly understands the command, he should be able to stay in the *sit* position for several minutes at a time.

Heel

I view the *heel* as an absolute necessity, because it makes walking with your Rottie an enjoyable pursuit rather than a painful or exasperating experience. *Heeling* is simply a controlled walk, and every Rottweiler should be required to perform it. An untrained Rottweiler often will surge ahead on the lead, pulling the owner along for a ride, or he may lag behind or veer off to the sides whenever he finds an interesting scent to follow. Such bad habits cannot be tolerated and must be stopped while the dog is young.

The first few minutes outside should be allotted for elimination and investigation. Once your Rottie loses that initial thrill to be outside, you are ready to set off.

Your Rottweiler should always walk on your left side, his chest preferably in line with your knee. Hold the lead in your right hand and use your left to supply corrective jerks when needed.

1. Begin with your Rottie in a *sit.*

2. Step off with your *left* foot, commanding, *"Festus, heel!"* as you move forward. If he does not follow you instinctively, give the leash a tug to start him forward. Remove the pressure from the lead whenever your Rottie responds and remains in proper position.

3. Walk at a pace that is comfortable *for you* and jerk the lead only if he strays from position. Make your snaps quick and firm and repeat, *"Festus, heel!"* with each correction. Praise him as soon as he responds, using a pleasant tone and *"Good boy!"* Repeat the praise every now

and then as you are moving if he remains in position, but don't overdo it, as this can interfere with his concentration and confuse him about what you are praising.

If you aspire to any obedience competition, your Rottie will be required to sit at your side whenever you stop. Many owners do not require this of their dogs, but it is a good action to ingrain because it always keeps the dog in proximity and tight control. In the beginning you will need to issue the *sit* command whenever you stop, but as he becomes adept at the procedure, the *sit* will become automatic and no verbal command should be needed.

Whenever he strays significantly from the proper position, you must break this pattern by stopping for the *sit.* If not, you will be applying continuous pressure from the lead on the dog's neck. In this way the choke collar will become meaningless and frustrating to the dog, and possibly physically damaging. The choke collar is to be used sparingly to regain his attention and bring about a correction in the form of a sharp, upward tug. It is to be used only when needed and should be released immediately. It should never be used to inflict pain! Rottweilers are extremely muscular around the neck and oftentimes are impervious to the snap of the standard choke chain. If this is the case with your dog, you should consult a professional trainer for guidance on selecting a more effective training collar that is appropriate for the breed.

The initial *heeling* lessons should last only 10 to 15 minutes. When your Rottie becomes more adept and no longer needs the frequent corrective *sits,* you can lengthen the *heeling* lessons as energy and interest permit. Once he becomes accomplished at *heeling,* your time together during walks will be infinitely more pleasurable. You must also take care to instruct and proof your Rottie on how to react to other people and animals that he may encounter during these walks.

Learning to heel takes time, and you can count on your Rottweiler to frequently lose interest in remaining at your side. Every time the dog breaks from position, stop and place him in a *sit.* You should not have to endure continually snapping the dog back into position. By placing the dog in a *sit,* you allow him to succeed at a task he already knows, and therefore he can be praised. Without this break, there can be a lot of leash corrections and not much praise administered. Resorting to the *sit* will help the heeling practice continue rather than break down into confusion on the dog's part and anger on the trainer's. Once your Rottie has successfully completed the *sit,* step off again with *"Festus, heel!"* and repeat the procedure.

Come

Once your Rottie has adapted to the sound of his name, a puppy will almost always happily come when called in anticipation of something pleasant. As he matures, he encounters a few unpleasant experiences and his responses sometimes become more reluctant (I call this the "What's in it for me?" syndrome). The *come* teaches your Rottie to control his urges and obey his master's call regardless of the circumstances, without hesitation.

Rottweilers will instinctively respond to the sound of their owner's voice and seek it out, and this is a valuable tool when training for the *come*.

1. Begin the training period with some pleasant play. Your Rottie should be roaming on a long lead or rope (20 feet [6.1 m] or more works best) in the practice yard, with the trainer holding the lead but maintaining only minimal tension.

2. Once the dog is relaxed and preoccupied, command, *"Festus, come!"* and lightly tug the lead to start the dog moving toward you. Praise when he *begins* to move. Have him come directly to you and place him in a *sit*.

3. If he does not respond to the tug, give another and repeat, *"Festus, come!"* Should your Rottie stubbornly resist, repeat the command once more and calmly reel the dog in by slowly retracting the cord.

4. Once he reaches your side, place him in a *sit*.

5. Release with *"Good boy!"* and let him roam once more.

Practice the *come* intermittently, enforcing the command with a tug on the lead whenever he fails to move immediately toward you. Test your Rottie on the *come* no more than once or twice each training session, but do not hesitate to use the *come* at various times throughout the day when you *really want* him to return to your side. Do not use the command if you are not in a position to enforce it, however. The main points to remember are that you must praise your Rottie highly when he comes when called, and that you must never allow him to ignore the command.

The owner must use this command responsibly. *Never command your Rottie to come to you and then punish him when he arrives!* When you see your dog doing something wrong, *go to him* and administer the correction. Should you command the dog to come and then punish him when he gets there, you almost certainly will ruin your chances of having a dog that will return to you instantly when called.

Down

The *down* is a very useful, sometimes lifesaving command. Do not attempt to teach your Rottweiler the *down* until he is reliably performing the *sit* and the *stay*.

1. Begin by placing the dog in a *sit*, with you kneeling by his side.

2. As you command your Rottie to *"Down,"* grab his front legs near the body, gently lift them from the floor, and lower him to the floor.

3. Once down, command him to *"Down, stay!"* (Remove the *stay* part of the command as soon as he begins to understand the concept.) A very responsive dog can be enticed to drop his front down through just hand motions beginning under the dog's chin and arching down to the floor and out in front of his paws. It is useful to incorporate a down motion with your hand at the time of the command, especially if you intend to continue into obedience competition.

4. Praise with *"Good boy"* once he reaches and remains in the prone position.

5. Rest your left hand on the dog's back to deter him from rising if he appears ready to pop back up.

6. Release your Rottie after a few seconds by motioning upward with your hand and gently tugging the lead. He should then return to the *sit* position.

The downward movement is the concept that he needs to learn, and this must be clearly differentiated from the *stay*. Do not make your Rottie remain in the *down* position too long at first, and be sure he remains lying on all fours. He is to be alert in this position, not sprawled over the floor.

Practice the *down* several times each day. As the downward drop becomes more familiar, try issuing the command and just slapping the floor with the palm of your hand to get him moving down. If you still encounter a reluctant response, try placing the lead under your left foot, keeping it rather taut, and as you command *"Down!"* add a slight pressure on his shoulders to get him moving down.

Once the *down* becomes a natural movement for your Rottie, teach him to lie down on the lead from various positions (such as in front of you or from a distance). When working indoors, practice the *down* off the leash. Never accept a sloppy performance once the lead is removed, however. Often, your Rottie may not feel compelled to obey once he realizes that the lead is no longer attached. Such behavior is, of course, unacceptable.

Down-Stay

One of the most effective methods of controlling your Rottweiler in various situations is through use of the *down-stay,* an exercise combining two of the commands discussed above. With practice your Rottie will remain in a *down-stay* for 30 minutes or more, enabling the master to remove the dog from those activities he is not invited to participate in or to keep him from getting underfoot without having to lock him up. The *down-stay* teaches your Rottie self-discipline and enforces the trainer's position as leader.

1. Select a spot that is out of the way, yet not secluded, and tell the dog to *"Down, stay."* The owner should remain nearby to monitor him but should not pay too much attention to him during the process. Begin with *stays* of a few minutes and gradually increase the time, but vary the length of the *stays* so that he cannot anticipate when the exercise will be finished.

2. During the initial attempts your Rottweiler undoubtedly will try to break the *stay.* As soon as he *begins* to move, tell him, *"No, stay!"* and replace him.

3. End the *down-stay* with an *"Okay"* and an upward sweep of the hand, and follow with lots of praise. This exercise requires a ton of self-control, and it does not come easily to a Rottweiler, but through practice and praise it can be mastered. Its usefulness cannot be overstated.

It is perfectly acceptable to let your Rottie sleep during the *down-stay* as long as he remains where he was placed when he awakens. You need to formally complete the exercise, however, to be sure it has an impact, so wake him by tapping your foot near his head or gently slapping the floor in front of his head when it is time to release him.

Training Problems

Various problems can arise during training that interfere with the learning process. Your dog may not be able to adapt to the training method you have selected. Finding the solution to a training problem generally is a matter of trial and error, and, most of all, patience and perseverance. With a breed as assertive as the Rottweiler, there is often a need to call upon the expertise of a trained professional.

Possible Causes

When you encounter a training problem, step back a bit and evaluate your teaching technique. Are your commands clear, concise, and consistent? Are you rushing the dog rather than giving him ample time to learn? Do you speak

in a firm, authoritative tone, or do you shout, scold, or whine? Do you praise him for every success?

By observing your Rottie's behavior and body language during training you may get some clues about the cause of the problems.

• *Is he easily distracted?* You may need to train in a more secluded training site and see if his concentration improves. Alternatively, your Rottie may be too young to begin formal training.

• *Are the training problems a new occurrence or a constant?* A sudden disinterest in training or confusion in a male can sometimes be caused by a local bitch in heat. A temporary learning plateau commonly occurs for both dogs and bitches during the fifth or sixth week of training that makes it appear as if your Rottie has forgotten all he has learned. This odd phenomenon generally passes in a week or so.

• *Is the dog ill?* A Rottweiler that is reluctant to move freely or jump may be showing the early signs of hip dysplasia, panosteitis, or another medical problem (see "If Your Rottweiler Gets Sick," page 83). A Rottie in pain also may reflect this in excessive aggressiveness.

If he shows any of these tendencies, have him examined thoroughly by a veterinarian.

Control

Control is an absolute must when dealing with a Rottweiler. If you feel things are not progressing well, consult a professional trainer who is experienced with this breed. Many times a new approach or technique that the dog will understand or like better will correct the problem. Sometimes the owner needs instruction in how to keep his interest or discipline him effectively.

Training setbacks are inevitable and must be countered with patience and repetition. The owner of a Rottweiler can expect a certain amount of feistiness on the part of the dog, for it is in his nature. A danger arises if an owner counters each problem with anger and hostile treatment, as this can have a detrimental effect on the future training of your Rottie. On the other hand, if an owner despairs and gives in to the will of a Rottweiler, there is the added danger that the dog will end up uncontrollable and aggressive. Should things deteriorate, *seek help from a professional.* It is money well spent.

FEEDING AND GROOMING YOUR ROTTWEILER

Rottweilers are large, active dogs with high energy needs. Most have great appetites and will eat whatever they are given. Feeding such dogs sounds like a simple—although potentially expensive—process, but because feeding does have a direct effect on a dog's health and longevity, it should not be taken lightly.

Feeding

Ask 50 experienced Rottweiler owners and breeders what the best diet for the breed is and you will probably get 50 variations of the methods described below. But all would agree that there are a few basic rules that help protect your Rottweiler from problems related to feeding:

• First and foremost, keep your Rottie on the lean side throughout his life. This is especially important for a Rottie puppy, as rapid growth can heighten his chance of developing some of the breed's genetic disorders. Research has shown that lean Rottweilers often live longer—as much as two years—than overweight ones. Excess weight can aggravate joint problems in adults and robs the dog of his vitality.

You should be able to easily feel but not see all his ribs. If you can count them by looking, he is too thin. If you have to feel down for them, he's too heavy.

• Wash all food and water bowls daily in hot, soapy water to prevent the growth of bacteria.

• Have ample amounts of clean, fresh water available at all times, especially during periods of hot weather.

• Remove the water bowl at night if the dog is having housebreaking problems.

• Vary the diet only when absolutely necessary.

• Introduce a new food slowly, over one or two weeks, gradually mixing the new in with the old, to avoid digestive upset.

• Bring along a supply of the dog's usual food when traveling or whenever the dog must be kenneled so that it does not have to suddenly adjust to a new food.

Types of Food

There are various types of food you can feed your Rottweiler. Some dog owners select one type; others use a combination. The task is to present a daily ration that is nutritionally complete and balanced and suited to your dog's particular lifestyle and age. Elderly dogs may need an easily digested formula, whereas overweight or inactive dogs will require a low-calorie diet. Growing puppies and pregnant or lactating bitches require a diet high in protein and calories. Which type of food is best? Which brand is best? The owner must take many fac-

tors into consideration, and then do some comparative shopping when making this decision.

It should be stressed that a Rottie puppy must be fed a diet that has been specifically designed for large-breed puppies. Research has shown that diet—especially overfeeding, paired with overexercising—favors or complicates the development of canine hip dysplasia (HD), a debilitating disease that leads to pain and limited mobility in an affected dog (see "If Your Rottweiler Gets Sick," page 83). Overexercising, overfeeding, and/or feeding a Rottie a diet with improper ratios of certain vitamins and minerals (especially calcium and phosphorous) will increase the risk of HD, so don't take the choice of food lightly! Your Rottweiler will arrive at his adult height and weight at about two years; there is no need to rush his growth along. Rottie breed-

══════ TIP ══════

Hard or Crunchy Food

- Giving your Rottweiler a hard or crunchy food, such as carrots or a sturdy knuckle-bone, can help to keep his teeth clean because they will scrape away some of the tartar that accumulates along the surface.
- Care must be taken when choosing bones, because an inappropriate bone can splinter when chewed. Nylon or rawhide bones are the safest choice among the commercial products. Check where the product is made, however, as many are imported from countries that do not carefully monitor pet products.

ers have a saying: "Grow your puppies slowly." This will help produce a healthier adult.

Dry Food. A high-quality dry food (commonly referred to as kibble) is the most popular type of prepared dog food. On average, an adult Rottweiler will eat anywhere from two to six cups of kibble a day. Given that a 40-pound (18.2-kg) bag of high-quality dry food costs approximately $40–$50, the expense can be considerable over a lifetime!

There are many brands and formulas of dry food on the market. Choose one that is labeled "complete and balanced" by the Association of American Feed Control Officials (AAFCO), which means that the pet-food manufacturer has conducted a feeding trial that followed the guidelines established by the AAFCO for levels of protein, fat, minerals, and fat- and water-soluble vitamins. Read labels thoroughly and compare one brand against another. Try to avoid products that contain chemical preservatives, such as BHT or BHA, or dyes, which can cause allergies.

The premium meat-meal-based kibbles sold in pet shops are designed to offer a stable mixture from batch to batch that is nutritionally complete, easily digested, and formulated to help produce a firm stool. Although these premium dry foods may cost more on a per-pound basis, the superior quality guarantees that your Rottie will fulfill all his nutritional requirements without having to eat massive amounts of the food or receive supplementation.

Active dogs such as Rottweilers need a diet that can fulfill their energy demands. Because

dry food products may be low on fat content, owners sometimes try to boost the fat by adding approximately one-quarter can of canned food or several tablespoons of cottage cheese to the kibble. Cut back on the amount of kibble if some additions are made.

To make the kibble more palatable for the dog, and possibly help prevent a digestive condition commonly called bloat or GDV (gastric dilatation and volvulus—see "If Your Rottweiler Gets Sick," page 83) you should saturate dry food with warm water until it is soupy and let it stand for several minutes. Stir the remaining "gravy" around the kibble before serving. By preparing the kibble in this way, it will absorb most of the moisture and expand before the dog eats it. It is also wise to feed your Rottie only after he has been inactive for 30 minutes and to keep his activities limited for one hour after eating.

Canned Food. Many owners mistakenly believe that because canned food is more expensive than dry food, it must be better. Too much protein in a diet is not better than just enough protein. Most canned dog foods contain more than 75 percent water. The remaining components are often meat by-products, soy fillers, vitamins, minerals, and, frequently, artificial coloring and preservatives.

When reading the label of a canned dog food, bear in mind that the first four ingredients are the primary components. Avoid products that contain high levels of red dye, salt, corn syrup or sugar, and preservatives. The high water level and additives in canned food can have a diuretic effect on many Rotties.

Canned food should make up no more than one-quarter of a Rottweiler's daily intake, and it should be mixed with a high-quality dry food

for best results. The canned food products formulated for the various stages of life are most recommended. Because canned food is highly palatable, dogs needing to gain or maintain weight can be fed higher levels of this food. Conversely, overweight dogs should be given only limited amounts of canned food.

Semimoist Food. Most dog food found in pouches or shaped as pork chops or hamburgers are touted for their convenience, but they are the most expensive type of dog food and the least nutritious. Avoid them. They are loaded with additives and preservatives, often with high levels of sugar and salt. Semimoist products are highly processed and high in calories, and have been linked to allergic reactions—from skin biting and scratching to hyperactivity—in response to the preservatives.

Raw Diet. A growing number of dog owners have adopted a "raw" diet, commonly called the BARF diet (alternately defined as "Bones and Raw Foods" or "Biologically Appropriate Raw Food"). This diet does not contain any grain products, as necessary carbohydrates are obtained from fresh fruits and vegetables. Raw lamb, chicken, and beef provide the protein as well as many minerals from the bones. Such a diet should be undertaken only after much research and consultation with a veterinarian or nutritionist for guidelines on all dietary requirements.

The Feeding Process

Rottweilers are enthusiastic eaters, and the owner will want to ensure that this is a controlled experience and a simple process. If handled properly, the daily meals should not overly excite your Rottie or cause him to growl protectively once given his meal.

Where to Feed Your Rottweiler

Your dog must be allowed to eat his meal in peace. He should not be rushed or made to feel nervous. An out-of-the-way place is most appropriate; expecting your Rottie to eat in the middle of the kitchen at the busiest time of day undoubtedly will cause him to constantly monitor the movement throughout the area and worry about whether his food is going to be taken away. Bad habits, such as an aggressive attitude toward the food, can develop in response to the dog's anxiety. This habit cannot be tolerated. A Rottweiler must be trained from an early age to allow his master to pick up and remove his food, if necessary, without protest. Moving the bowl to various places in a room will keep the dog from getting too routinized and will promote healthy eating patterns. An anxious dog often will devour its food quickly, which can result in digestive problems, vomiting, and possibly a life-threatening condition known as "bloat" (see "Gastric Dilatation and Volvulus," page 95).

When to Feed

The age of the dog is the main factor in determining when to feed him each day. Puppies require several small meals a day, until approximately four to six months of age, when they can be switched to two. Your Rottie should be given ample time to eat his meal. Fifteen minutes usually is sufficient. Pick up and discard any food that remains after this time.

Lack of Interest in Eating

Rottweilers rarely are problem eaters, so a sudden lack of interest in eating usually is caused by a health or dental problem. If your Rottie refuses his food, discard it and do not offer a replacement until the next scheduled meal. If the problem persists for more than a few meals, he should be examined by a veterinarian.

Chewing

Every Rottie puppy has the urge to chew when teething and shedding his first teeth, and again when his back molars are emerging. Many owners are fooled into thinking that chewing will then end, but, in fact, a dog will chew throughout his life. The amount of chewing will vary from dog to dog, and is affected by age, temperament, training, and level of exercise (that is, boredom). To put it simply, Rotties are big chewers.

Chewing hard substances can be beneficial, as it helps remove some of the tartar buildup that has accumulated on the teeth. Many Rottweilers find it a pleasurable pastime. Some Rottweilers chew to release tension, often causing extensive and expensive damage to household goods or even the house! A Rottweiler that is left alone for long stretches of time often placates his loneliness by chewing.

CHECKLIST

Chewing

1. Most Rottweilers enjoy rawhide bones, but they can usually devour them in short order. This can become quite expensive and may pose some health problems, as large chunks of undigested rawhide can sometimes cause constipation or blockage.
2. Nylon bones are long lasting and sturdy, but many dogs don't like them.
3. Hard beef or veal bones, such as from the knuckle, should be given only occasionally, as they can be constipating and abrasive to the tooth enamel if the dog is an energetic chewer.
4. Plastic toys should be given only when the dog is being supervised, as these can be torn apart and swallowed, leading to choking.

It is a pretty safe bet to say that every Rottweiler will find something to chew that he shouldn't, especially from puppyhood through three years of age. Because there is no simple, foolproof method to stop chewing, the owner's best recourse to minimize the losses is to confine your Rottie in a crate whenever he cannot be supervised and to always have a suitable chew toy available.

The owner must let the dog know exactly what *may* and *may not* be chewed upon. Be realistic: You cannot expect a Rottie to understand that it is okay to chew on an old slipper but not on the new pair. Never allow a puppy to chew on electric wires, as the resulting shock could prove fatal. Your Rottweiler must also be taught to stay away from household plants; some are poisonous if ingested.

When you catch your Rottie with a forbidden object in his mouth, remove it from his clutches and shake it in front of his head as you say, *"No chew!"* in a stern voice. Immediately give him something he is allowed to chew. In this way you will help him connect your displeasure with his chewing of the object. If he continues to chew, you may need to try a commercial spray designed to leave an unpleasant taste in his mouth, but be sure to choose one that is prepared from nontoxic herbs and spices.

Grooming

Care of the Coat

The Rottweiler has a coarse, dense outercoat that lies flat to his body, as well as an undercoat that must be present on the neck and thighs while not showing through the outer coat. The amount of undercoat is influenced by climatic conditions and seasonal changes and serves as a layer of insulation against the cold and heat. The Rottweiler is susceptible to skin allergies, so be sure to have a veterinarian check his coat if you notice any excessive scratching or biting at the skin.

Although the Rottweiler does not lose excessive amounts of hair, it will shed much of his coat twice a year to help adjust to the changing seasons. During the rest of the year, the coat will shed a moderate amount, and it needs to be brushed once or twice a week with a medium-to-firm bristle brush or a hound glove (a grooming glove with short bristles in the palm that help remove dead hairs). These routine

brushings will remove the dead hairs that cling to the coat and in the process will clean the skin and the shafts of the living hair. The Rottweiler is a natural breed, and his coat is never to be cut or trimmed (although show dogs often have stray hairs around their feet tidied and their whiskers trimmed for competition).

The following are some helpful hints for cleaning your Rottie's coat should it become soiled with hard-to-remove substances:

• *Chewing gum:* Rub the gum with some peanut butter, leave it on for a few minutes, then ease the gum out of the coat using a wide-toothed comb.

• *Oil-based paint:* Let it harden, and then scissor off the hair. Never use turpentine, kerosene, or other solvents near the skin.

• *Tar (on feet or between toes):* Carefully clip off as much affected hair as possible, then soak the area with vegetable oil. Let the oil remain for several hours, and then shampoo.

• *Grease:* Dust the area with cornstarch, let it absorb for one hour, and then brush it out, shampoo, and rinse.

• *Odors:* Bathe the area in warm, sudsy water and rinse thoroughly. For powerful odors, pour a solution of vinegar and water over your Rottie's back and let it dry in. Repeat the process if necessary.

Bathing

The Rottweiler should be bathed as infrequently as possible, usually only when the dog becomes excessively dirty or comes in contact with a foul substance. Given a proper dose of brushing, the Rottweiler's coat should remain clean year-round and should not give off a "doggy" odor.

When bathing is needed, use a very mild soap designed especially for dogs—not products for humans, which are too harsh and drying for a dog's coat. Wet the coat thoroughly, working the water down to the skin. Begin with the head and proceed down, being very careful that water and shampoo do not get into your Rottie's eyes and ears. Once he is fully lathered, rinse the coat well with lots of warm water. The soap must be totally removed from the undercoat or your dog's skin may become irritated and he may develop dandruff. During cold weather be sure to towel him dry or blow-dry him from a 6-inch (15 cm) distance so that he is not exposed to any cold air until the undercoat is totally dry.

Care of the Nails

Rottweilers need a lot of outside exercise and activity, and through this most get enough exposure to rough pavement to keep the nails naturally worn down. During the weekly grooming session, owners should inspect their Rottie's nails to be sure they do not need to be trimmed, as overgrown nails can impede the normal placement of the foot and affect his gait.

Few Rottweilers like having their feet held for any length of time. To counteract this natural reluctance and instinct to pull away, begin getting your Rottie puppy used to having this area touched by regularly playing with his feet and toes while petting and grooming. You can later try massaging the foot pads. This preparation will be valuable if the nails ever need to be clipped. It also enforces your position as master.

If you are inexperienced with clipping nails, have your veterinarian show you this simple procedure at your Rottie's regular checkup. Once instructed, you can handle this process at home when it is required. Use a specially designed "guillotine" clipper when trimming your Rottie's nails, not a product designed for humans. The proper equipment can be purchased from pet stores, grooming parlors, and veterinarians. Cut only the outer tip of the nail, as cutting too close to the vein (called the "quick") is very painful for the dog and can cause bleeding. Once the nail is shortened to the proper length, you may need to smooth the surface with a few brushes of an emery board. If you cut too close to the quick and the nail bleeds, apply pressure by holding a piece of cotton gauze over the nail or use a styptic pencil. Once the bleeding stops, dab the nail with a mild antiseptic.

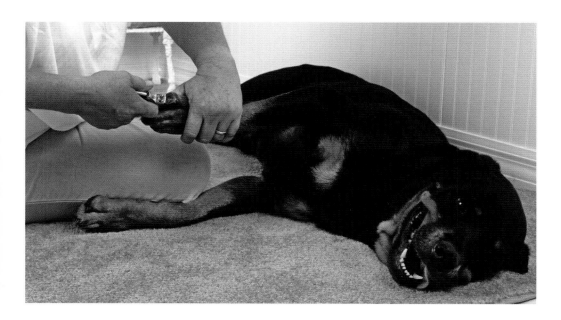

IF YOUR ROTTWEILER GETS SICK

The most successful method for safeguarding your Rottweiler's health is through monitoring the dog's outward appearance at home and backing this up with an annual physical examination by a veterinarian.

As is typical with many large breeds, Rottweilers have a life expectancy of around 9 to 11 years. To keep your Rottie as healthy as possible for as long as possible, there are some health problems that you should be aware of, and you should have your dog professionally evaluated at least yearly. At annual examinations, the veterinarian will assess your dog's general condition, test for internal parasites, and determine if he needs any vaccinations. Through routine inspections such as these, you have a better chance of catching any potential health problems early, and cure rates are considerably higher when illnesses are diagnosed in the beginning stages.

It also is vital that you bring your Rottie in for professional care if you notice such symptoms as sudden weight loss or gain, drinking excessive amounts of water, lethargy, persistent vomiting or diarrhea, or change in the coat.

A proper diagnosis by a veterinarian is essential because these symptoms can be associated with many disorders. Although most common illnesses are easily cured, many health problems can become life-threatening when left to "run their course" by slow-acting owners.

Evaluating Your Dog's Health

A good way to keep close tabs on your Rottweiler's outward condition is by performing a quick inspection of the dog during routine grooming sessions. Begin by running your hands over the dog's entire body and feeling for anything unusual, such as cuts, swelling, cysts, calluses, or areas that seem painful to your Rottie when touched. The Rottweiler's dark coat may hide any visible signs of skin problems, so be sure to work your fingers down to the skin. You should then turn to the head and begin a more thorough evaluation.

Eyes

Healthy eyes should be bright and shiny; they should not appear inflamed, bloodshot, or overly tear laden. The inner lining of the eyelids should be moist and pink, and the whites of the eyes should not show any yellowing. A slight discharge in the corner of the eyes is normal and can be cleared away easily with a damp, lint-free cloth. Do not use cotton balls, as these can leave tiny fibers behind in the eye. A clear discharge usually is related to the drainage of the tears and can be exacerbated by minor irritations and inflammations such as conjunctivitis. Should this discharge become excessive or change color to cloudy or yellowish, or if your Rottie seems bothered by light, paws at the eye, or blinks excessively, and the eye is red, consult your veterinarian as an infection may be present.

It is not uncommon for a Rottweiler to get a minor scratch on the eye while moving through underbrush. This generally will heal on its own without requiring medical attention. Should a burr or small object get into the eye, immediately irrigate the eye with some warm water or carefully dab the corner of the eye with a soft cloth. Should a foreign object become lodged, seek immediate veterinary care, as probing for it may seriously injure the eye.

Every Rottweiler that is to be used in a breeding program should be examined annually by a certified veterinary ophthalmologist until at least eight years of age, because there are several hereditary diseases common with this breed, including progressive retinal atrophy and central progressive retinal atrophy. Rotties found to be clear of the major genetic disorders

will be issued a certificate by the Canine Eye Registration Foundation (CERF).

It is estimated that approximately 8 percent of Rottweilers tested for eye disease are found to have cataracts—a condition where the lens that is used for focusing clouds and obstructs proper vision. It can lead to blindness. Cataracts have been detected in Rotties as young as 18 months, although it is most common between four and six years of age. This can occur in one or both eyes, plus it can happen over a matter of weeks or slowly over several years. Surgery by a veterinary ophthalmologist to remove the cataract and replace it with an artificial lens is successful in more than 90 percent of the cases. Afflicted Rottweilers should not be bred, because this condition is often hereditary.

Rottweilers may also be afflicted by a genetic eye disorder known as *entropion*, which is a congenital defect of the eyelids where the lid rolls in, bringing the eyelashes in contact with the cornea. Symptoms are a constant blinking or scratching at the eyes. This painful condition can be heightened by dust or debris in the eye. Similarly, *ectropion*—when the eyelid rolls outward—sometimes occurs. Surgery is usually required to fix these problems.

Ears

Because Rottweilers have pendant ears, the owner will need to regularly check and clean inside them every few weeks. A dog with ear problems will constantly shake his head or rub his ears with his paws or on the ground. If there is an excessive amount of visible earwax, redness, swelling, or a foul odor coming from the ear canal, a veterinarian's attention is required.

Never probe down into the dog's ear canal, as this can be extremely painful and cause great damage. To help remove the normal buildup of wax and dirt in the outer ear, pull up the ear and swab the easily accessible area with a cotton ball wet with a little warm water or with a wet cloth wrapped around your forefinger. Ointments made specially for cleaning the ear can be purchased from pet shops, grooming parlors, or your veterinarian if cleanliness is a continual problem. Avoid oily compounds, as they may attract and retain dirt.

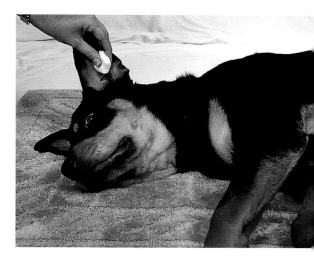

If you suspect that the inner ear is clogged with wax, bring your Rottie to your veterinarian for a thorough cleaning. If the problem is chronic, you can ask for instruction on how to perform this procedure at home.

Should your dog wince with pain when his ears are touched, an infection may be present. An inflammation of the ear, called *otitis*, can be treated topically or with antibiotics. This condition can have several causes, such as parasitic mites or a bacterial or yeast infection. Allergies often are a root cause as well. Large deposits of black or reddish brown earwax commonly are found with ear disorders, so seek veterinary assistance at the onset of the problem.

Occasionally your Rottweiler may get a minor abrasion on the earflap. The most important task is to keep the afflicted area clean to avoid infection. Your veterinarian can advise you about what best to apply if you find a scratched or abraded area. Should you suspect that an object has somehow become lodged in the ear, seek immediate veterinary attention and *do not attempt to probe the ear yourself.*

Tooth Care

Few Rottweilers eat a diet that contains enough natural abrasives to remove the tartar, or plaque, that builds up over the years at the gum line. Although encouraging your dog to eat carrots and chew safe, hard bones will aid in tartar removal, this seldom is sufficient.

Unless conditioned, most adult Rotties are reluctant to have their teeth cleaned, so you must accustom him from puppyhood to allow you to gently clean his teeth with a soft child's toothbrush or a moistened gauze pad wrapped around your finger. A yellowing of the tooth exterior is common as your Rottie ages and often can be minimized by routine treatment. The teeth can be brushed once or twice a week with special dental products designed for dogs that can be purchased from veterinarians or pet stores.

Note: Do not use toothpaste made for humans on your dog; it can cause stomach upsets.

If discoloring remains despite weekly brushings, the teeth may need to be scaled by your veterinarian. Heavy deposits will need to be removed by ultrasonic scraping and the dog will need to be anesthetized.

Although cavities are seldom a problem for dogs, there are other conditions the owner

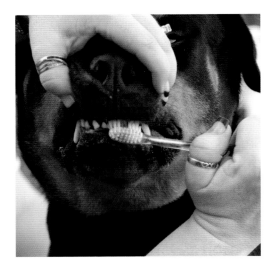

should be aware of. A sudden change in your Rottie's breath that lasts for more than a few days may indicate a problem with the teeth, tonsils, or throat. A loss of appetite could stem from tooth problems, as decayed teeth make it painful for him to eat. Inspect the teeth and gums for any obvious sign of infection, swelling, bleeding, or sensitivity to the touch. An abscessed tooth sometimes manifests itself as a boil-like growth on the cheek area. Your veterinarian should be informed as soon as you notice any of these conditions.

Occasional bad breath can be treated with several commercial products, which the dog chews and ingests. Most contain chlorophyll, which is a natural ingredient that helps promote fresh breath.

Feet

Working dogs, such as Rottweilers, give their legs and feet a considerable pounding in the course of a normal day. Consequently, these areas are susceptible to various minor injuries. If not accustomed to having their feet touched, Rottweilers will be reluctant to have them worked on. This can be avoided by routinely massaging his feet during play, starting when he is a puppy.

The pads of the feet should be inspected regularly and wiped with a clean, damp cloth whenever your Rottie is out in wet and cold weather. If he limps or favors a leg, check the foot for burrs, splinters, chewing gum, or stones that may have become embedded in and between the pads of the foot. If necessary, use sterile tweezers to carefully remove any object. Scratches and cuts on the pad are common. Nails can also be torn (see "Care of the Nails," page 81). For minor problems, a gentle cleaning with a mild antiseptic should be sufficient. An application of a little petroleum jelly often will soothe irritated feet.

A sudden limp or a furious case of licking the foot may indicate that your Rottie has been stung by an insect. Apply an ice compress to reduce or prevent swelling and ease the pain. Unless the dog shows signs of an allergic reaction (see "Stinging Insects," page 91), this discomfort should pass quickly.

If the dog indicates pain in the foot and there is no obvious cut or sting, there may be an injury to the bones or muscle tissue or an object may be embedded deeply in the foot pad. Hard at work or play, a Rottweiler may turn too sharply and suffer a muscle pull. Although rarely serious, these conditions require the expertise of a veterinarian for a proper diagnosis.

The foot pads require special attention during the winter months when your Rottweiler's feet may be exposed to the chemicals used to melt ice and snow. These compounds can be caustic to a dog's feet and skin. If you suspect that

your Rottie has walked on these chemicals, rinse his feet with warm, soapy water. Follow this with a thin layer of petroleum jelly. If these irritating chemicals are not removed from your Rottie's feet, he may try to lick them off. Ingesting such poisonous materials is extremely hazardous to a dog's digestive tract.

Legs and Elbows

Hip and elbow problems are, unfortunately, fairly common in Rottweilers. See "Hip and Elbow Dysplasia," page 96.

Vaccinations

During the first few weeks of a puppy's life he receives antibodies from his mother that protect him from various diseases. Once weaned, however, the puppy becomes susceptible to communicable diseases and must be protected by receiving a series of vaccinations. These are broken into two main categories: core (those that are always needed for potentially fatal diseases) and noncore (those that are needed only when your Rottie is at a high-risk of exposure to diseases, such as bordetella, parainfluenza, leptospirosis, and Lyme disease). The frequency of these vaccinations is a topic of great discussion by veterinarians, many of whom are now considering giving the "booster" shots every three years rather than annually, so you should discuss this with him or her on your first visit.

Most puppies receive their first immunizations at around seven to eight weeks of life, while they are still with their breeder. Until then, they have been naturally protected by antibodies received from their dam. The first shots usually include vaccinations for canine parvovirus (CPV), canine distemper virus (CDV), and canine adenovirus-2 (CAV). These first shots generally protect the dog for only a few weeks, so follow-up shots will be required for most core vaccines, on a schedule devised by your veterinarian.

A rabies vaccination should be administered no sooner than four months of age and again one year later. Don't have your dog get a rabies shot until at least four weeks after a CDV or CPV injection. Most states require rabies boosters every three years, but a few states still require shots annually. This is the only vaccine required by law, and you won't be able to board your Rottie or participate in training classes without it.

Like humans, a small percentage of dogs experience poor reactions to some vaccines. It is not uncommon for a Rottweiler to run a low-grade fever after a rabies shot, and rarely there can be nonimmediate reactions, including seizures, behavior problems, and skin disorders. Contact your veterinarian should your Rottie react in any way to his vaccinations. Similarly, let your veterinarian know beforehand if your Rottweiler has reacted negatively to previous shots or will be bred in the next four months.

Be sure to request all records of your dog's earliest shots from the breeder and pass this information along to your veterinarian.

Stool and Urine Samples

Your Rottie should have a fecal check for worms and intestinal disorders once a year. Obtaining a sample is as simple as picking up after your dog has eliminated and enclosing it in a plastic bag, making sure that the sample does not have plant matter or dirt clinging to it. Worms are very common in puppies, so ask the breeder if yours has already been tested or treated for worms. If he has, find out what type of worm the puppy was infected with, what medication was used to treat him, and how the puppy reacted to the medication. This background information may be helpful for the veterinarian should the puppy become reinfested at some later date.

Urine samples are usually collected by the veterinarian by the use of a catheter, but you can oftentimes collect it yourself, especially with a male. Only a few tablespoons of sample is needed. First thing in the morning or after a meal is your best chance. Follow behind your dog with a clean, closeable container, and place it midstream once he starts. For a female or reluctant male, you can also try using a well-washed, long-handled ladle to collect some urine and then pour it into a container. Leashing your Rottie often helps to keep him easily within reach.

If you are not going directly to the veterinarian after collecting your samples, they can be refrigerated for several hours.

Internal and External Parasites

With outdoor-loving dogs such as Rottweilers, parasites can be unfortunate facts of life. The owners' task is to keep a close watch on the dog's condition so that problems can be caught before they become severe. This is important especially during the warmer months, when infestations are more prevalent.

Worms

Worms are common in dogs, especially puppies. The most common are roundworms, whipworms, hookworms, and tapeworms. Severe infestations can be very debilitating and sometimes life-threatening. Symptoms include weight loss, weakness, a bloated stomach, diarrhea, dull coat, and a poor or voracious appetite. Many infected dogs will give little outward sign of the problem until heavily infested, which highlights the importance of having your Rottie checked for worms at his annual checkup.

Only a veterinarian can properly diagnose the type of worm and select the proper medication. Well-meaning owners should never routinely worm a dog using over-the-counter preparations, as this process can be very dangerous and has led to numerous poisonings.

Heartworm is a potentially fatal internal parasite that is spread primarily by infected mosquitoes. Each year your Rottie should be given a blood test to check for heartworms. If the test is negative, a *preventive* medication in the form of a pill or chew tab should be administered on a monthly basis throughout mosquito season (early spring until after a killing frost) in cooler regions or year-round in warmer climates to keep the dog free from infection. There are several types available, but all require a veterinary prescription.

Many infected dogs show few symptoms while the heartworms are maturing, which takes about six months. Early signs of infection may include coughing, especially after physical activity, and difficulty breathing. Heartworm infestations may cause all the typical signs of heart failure, including seizures, lethargy, weakness, and lack of appetite. Treatment varies with the size and

number of adult heartworms in the heart and major vessels and may require surgical intervention. Without prompt veterinary diagnosis and treatment, the infestation may be fatal.

Fleas

Fleas can make a Rottweiler's life miserable. They bite his skin, suck his blood, make him itch unbearably, and sometimes can infect him with tapeworms. The severity of an infestation usually depends on the local climate and the owner's diligence in detecting and ridding the fleas from the dog and his surroundings.

Some Rotties are hypersensitive to flea saliva and can truly suffer after just one bite, scratching to the point of hair loss and skin infection. The Rottweiler's dark coat can make detection difficult, so the owner should thoroughly and routinely inspect his skin along the belly and

inner thigh, especially if he is scratching or biting himself. For every flea you see, there are many more lurking in the egg, larval, and pupal stages in your dog's bedding and probably in your carpeting, furniture, and anywhere he commonly frequents. There, in eight to ten days, the next generation of pests will hatch.

The best way to prevent flea infestations is by placing a topical solution on his back. Various compounds are available by prescription, and some also treat ticks, mites, and other parasites. It must be reapplied at regular intervals. *Read the instructions carefully.* Although there are veterinary medications available that will quickly kill the fleas on an infested dog, these have no residual effect and are primarily used

to rid your dog of a new infestation before starting one of the long-term preventives.

If your Rottie is heavily infested, a bath with a flea dip will be needed. Many grooming parlors supply this service, or you can do it at home. Always use products designed solely for this purpose, and read all directions before beginning.

Once the dog has been cleared of fleas, you will have to make sure that the house, especially the dog's bedding, is also free of flea larvae. An insect bomb or "fogger" (available at most hardware stores and pet shops) will be needed to reach deep into the carpeting and small cracks where fleas may be developing. Be sure to use enough to cover the entire house.

Ticks

Ticks are parasites that feed on your dog's blood. They can cause a variety of medical problems, including Rocky Mountain spotted fever, Lyme disease, anemia, and even paralysis. If left untreated, Lyme disease leads to arthritis, exhaustion, severe headaches, and heart problems.

Although much more slow-moving than fleas, ticks are still not detected easily on Rottweilers, as they are merely a fraction of an inch when they enter the coat. Infestations commonly occur on the hindquarters and around the ears.

Once on a host, a tick buries its head into the dog's skin and is then implanted so that it can suck and live off your dog's blood. The tick will remain until it has drunk its fill, becoming engorged with blood and swelling to many times its normal size. At this point it will disengage itself, and may then lay a large quantity of eggs to perpetuate the cycle.

A tick must be removed carefully. It should not be simply ripped from the skin, and you should never try to burn a tick off your dog using a match or cigarette.

The proper way to remove a tick is to grasp it firmly, using tweezers placed as close to the skin as possible. It is advisable to wear protective gloves when removing a tick, to minimize human exposure to such conditions as Lyme disease. Apply firm but gentle upward pressure. *Do not twist.* An alternative method is to apply a tick dip, which can be purchased from most veterinarians or pet shops. This will, in effect, suffocate the tick and make it release its hold on the dog's skin. Once a tick has been removed, a small lump or swollen area may remain for several days.

Lice and Mites

Lice usually are spread through contact with an infested animal. Once on your dog, the lice deposit eggs that adhere to his hair. Some diligence on the part of the owner will be required, as lice infestations often are difficult to cure.

Several types of mites infect different areas of the dog and produce a condition generally called *mange*. Mites also can be transmitted to humans, so owners must treat afflicted animals quickly and effectively.

Although less common than flea and tick infestations, lice and mites can cause intense itching and uncontrollable scratching in afflicted dogs. This can cause extensive damage to your Rottie's coat and skin that may take a long time to heal, so it is important to catch skin problems in the early stages. If you notice a rash of bumps or pustules on the dog's skin, consult your veterinarian for a proper diagnosis and treatment.

Stinging Insects

Fortunately, most insect bites are minor discomforts for a dog, just as for humans. Signs of a bite are difficult to detect, especially when occurring in the black parts of the Rottweiler's coat. If you happen to witness your dog being stung, or you notice sudden limping, check the site and see if a stinger is still embedded. If it is, carefully remove it by scraping your fingernail or the side of a credit card across the base of the bite using a scooping motion. This will remove the stinger and limit the spread of the venom. If possible, apply ice or a cold compress to the area to reduce swelling.

Occasionally a Rottie will have an allergic reaction to a bite. Reactions will vary from dog to dog, depending on his level of sensitivity and the amount of venom received. A case of hives or localized swelling generally will subside in a matter of hours, with no lasting effect. Administering an over-the-counter antihistamine (as advised by your veterinarian) or a corticosteroid will relieve most allergic reactions. A more severe reaction, such as marked swelling or difficulty breathing, requires immediate veterinary attention.

If your Rottie has had an allergic reaction to stinging insects, consult with your veterinarian and devise a strategy for coping with future emergencies. Have the antidotes readily available at all times.

Common Health Problems

Throughout their lives, most Rottweilers—just like humans—will contract a few minor health problems. If handled properly, these disorders should pass quickly. However, because dogs obviously are unable to verbally communicate their discomforts, it is up to the owner to accurately assess the dog's condition and decide whether veterinary attention is required.

Vomiting

Vomiting can have many causes. Most incidents will pass in a day and often are related to a "dietary indiscretion"—that is, something he has eaten (such as grass or garbage). In simple cases, withhold food and water for 12 hours. If there haven't been any more episodes, offer him a drink of water and some soft, bland food, such as chicken mixed with rice. If he keeps this down, offer another small meal in four hours. He should be able to resume normal meals the following day.

Other causes of vomiting include eating too quickly, a change in diet, intolerance to a specific food, or food allergy. Vomiting can also be a symptom of a more dangerous disorder (such as heatstroke, liver or kidney disease, pancreatitis, heartworm). Severe, continued vomiting—especially when combined with obvious signs of distress, weakness, or blood or worms in the vomit—is very serious and requires an immediate trip to the veterinarian.

Many Rottweilers have a tendency to gulp their food. If they take in too much air along with the food, the meal may come right back out. The best solution for Rotties prone to this is to serve them several small meals a day, thereby limiting the amount of food in the stomach at any one time. Using an elevated dog feeder may also help. Continued, unproductive vomiting can be an emergency situation needing immediate care (see "Gastric Dilatation and Volvulus," page 95).

Gulping and then vomiting may also be related to nervousness on the dog's part about his food possibly being removed. If this is the case, the owner must reassure him that there is nothing to fear. A dog such as the Rottweiler must be responsive to his owner and must allow his meal to be removed, if necessary, without any aggressive or overly nervous reaction. Few people think to take a sample of the vomit with them when going to the veterinarian, but it can be very helpful. Being able to examine it for signs of blood, mucus, or bile can speed up a proper diagnosis.

Diarrhea

As with vomiting, most cases of diarrhea—or soft stool—are relatively mild. Diarrhea can result from a change in the dog's diet or water

supply, the dog eating something irritating or indigestible, a side effect of a medication, or even emotional upset.

Mild diarrhea usually can be treated at home by withholding food (but not water) for at least 12 to 24 hours. If symptoms seem to be abating, offer your Rottie several small, bland meals containing rice and chicken every few hours. If the condition does not recur, you can resume the normal diet in three days.

Should the condition worsen or continue for more than 48 hours, consult your veterinarian. Dehydration can occur quickly with persistent diarrhea. Immediate veterinary assistance is

needed if you notice a bloody discharge or if the condition is combined with vomiting and/or a high fever. Bring a sample of the dog's stool for examination if veterinary help is required.

Constipation

If your Rottweiler does not move his bowels in his normal pattern—straining without passing stool or passing hard stools for 24 hours—he may be constipated. Other symptoms include listlessness and loss of appetite. Occasionally, a constipated dog may vomit. This does not happen frequently in Rottweilers, so you should consult your veterinarian and let him or her decide whether it is a mild, passing case or something more serious.

Constipation occurs more often in older dogs or those that chew meat bones (the chips of which are indigestible and harden the stools). It can also occur after a sudden change of diet. Confining your Rottie for too long a time may also cause this problem, as he restrains his natural urges to eliminate until allowed outside. In such cases, the problem usually is temporary. If your veterinarian decides that your Rottweiler is prone to constipation, you will first be advised to add extra roughage to his normal diet to aid proper elimination. A few tablespoons of canned pumpkin (unsweetened) is a natural aid, as is adding a little oat bran to his meals. Should the condition linger, you may be instructed to give him a specified amount of mineral oil or a mild over-the-counter laxative aid such as Metamucil.

If you ever see the dog actively straining, crying out with pain, and not passing any excrement, seek professional care at once. The dog may have swallowed something that is now lodged in the intestinal tract, causing a life-threatening situation. Alternatively, constipation can be caused by a tumor, an enlarged prostate, or a hernia that may be interfering with the normal functioning of the intestines. Such situations are emergencies that require specialized veterinary care.

Impacted Anal Sacs

At the base of a dog's anus are two sacs that secrete a strong-smelling substance used by the dog as a scent marker. The anal sacs normally are emptied during the defecation process. However, if they are not cleared completely by the normal elimination process, they can become impacted and will require manual emptying.

The symptoms of impacted anal sacs include a constant licking of the area and/or dragging the anus across the ground or floor (this is often referred to as "scooting"). Check the dog carefully, as a dog may also scoot if some feces has collected in the anal hair. If the anal sacs appear full, seek veterinary assistance. The sacs will be manually expressed, and the fluid checked for pus or blood, which would indicate that an infection is present.

Diseases and Disorders

Although generally a hearty breed, Rottweilers are prone to various physical and behavioral issues over their lifetime, including allergies, epilepsy, overaggressiveness, and thyroid problems. The following are some major health concerns.

Cancer

Cancer is the number one killer of adult Rottweilers, with bone cancer being most frequent. It is important to have your veterinarian inspect and/or remove any suspicious lumps, unhealed sores, or moles you may find.

Gastric Dilatation and Volvulus (GDV)

Often known as bloat or gastric torsion, GDV is a life-threatening condition where excess gas or fluid causes the stomach to swell and twist where it attaches to the esophagus and duodenum. It can be caused by taking in too much air by gulping down food, overeating, drinking too much water after eating, and/or exercise right after a meal. Symptoms include unproductive vomiting, a hunched posture, difficult breathing, a tight stomach to the touch, and anxiousness. Immediate veterinary care is essential, as surgery will be required.

Rottweilers that typically gulp their food or drink large amounts of water at one time are most susceptible to GDV. Water intake should be closely monitored, and the Rottie should receive several small meals a day rather than one or two.

Heart Disease

The most common heart disorder in Rottweilers is sub-aortic stenosis (SAS), a congenital heart defect of abnormal tissue below the aortic valve that obstructs blood flow. The heart is forced to work harder than normal, producing a murmur. Afflicted dogs should be evaluated by a veterinary cardiologist, who will grade the severity as mild, moderate, or severe. Rottweilers with mild SAS will be able to live a normal life, whereas a moderate rating will mean limits in exercise and heat exposure and treatment with medications, primarily beta blockers to keep the heart from overworking. Dogs with severe SAS may be prone to fainting, shortness of breath,

and overall weakness, and occasionally surgery will be performed to remove the restriction. The Orthopedic Foundation for Animals (OFA) has a congenital heart registry and issues certificates for those Rottweilers deemed to be free of the disease, to help breeders eliminate SAS through selective breeding.

Hip and Elbow Dysplasia

Hip dysplasia (HD) is a potentially crippling developmental disease that is found in Rottweilers, as well as most of the medium and large breeds that undergo rapid growth early in life. HD is a malformation of the hip joint that produces an improper fit of the hip socket and the femur bone. Constant friction caused by movement in an afflicted hip slowly wears the joint down as the dog ages, ultimately leading to pain when walking or during sudden movement. The first clinical signs of the disease generally do not appear until the dog is two to three years old, unless the Rottweiler puppy is severely afflicted. A palpation exam by your veterinarian while the puppy is five or six months of age can often turn up some joint laxity before it is evident on X-rays.

Although genetics plays an important role in HD, environmental factors also can affect its onset. Improper nutrition, overfeeding, and/or overexercising during the first year or two of life can drastically increase the incidence of HD in Rottweilers. Because HD is primarily heredi-tary, the best way to eliminate the problem is by breeding only those dogs that do not have a predisposition for the disease. Every Rottweiler intended for breeding should be X-rayed at 24 months of age for signs of HD. Specialists from the Orthopedic Foundation for Animals (OFA) will evaluate the X-rays and then issue a certifi-cate that rates the condition of the hips. Only those Rottweilers certified as clear of the prob-lem should be used in any breeding program. Rottweilers with mild cases of HD are usually treated with pain-reducing medication, and there are several surgical procedures available, based on severity.

Like hip dysplasia, elbow dysplasia is a hered-itary disease that afflicts some Rottweilers. It is a malformation of the joints in the elbow, diag-nosed by X-ray evaluation. Afflicted Rotties will often have an abnormal gait and pain when moving and rising and may stand with their feet rotated outward. Pain medication and/or surgery may be required. As with hip dysplasia, only those dogs with a passing evaluation by the OFA should be used in breeding plans.

Osteochondrosis Dissecans (OCD)

OCD is a disease where abnormally thick car-tilage affects the joints and leads to lameness.

OCD is found mainly in the shoulder joint, but it also afflicts the elbow and hock. If caught early, anti-inflammatories and painkillers, as well as severely restricted amounts of exercise, may alleviate the condition in several months. Severe cases will need surgery to remove the lesions.

Panosteitis

Panosteitis is sometimes referred to as "Rottie growing pains." Rottweiler puppies—predomi-nately males between the age of 4 and 18 months—sometimes exhibit lameness and pain in their shoulders, legs, and/or feet. It often comes and goes, rotates limbs, and can last for weeks or months at a time. The cause of this disorder is unknown, but once diagnosed via X-ray, the outcome is very good with crate rest and perhaps a course of anti-inflammatory drugs, such as Rimadyl.

Separation Anxiety

Rottweilers may be big, but they are also sensitive and people-oriented. Many do not like being alone. Separation anxiety can develop in your Rottie, often resulting in such destructive behaviors as digging and scratching at the doors and windows, barking or howling inces-santly, or soiling the house. These are acts of panic, not your Rottie trying to get back at you. This most often happens to Rotties that are suddenly alone after being accustomed to con-tinual human companionship, after a change of routine (moving, a new work schedule, or the death or sudden absence of family member), or following some sort of trauma (an injury or even a stay in a boarding kennel). The most effective way to prevent or mitigate separation anxiety is to make your departures and returns low key, to the point of almost ignoring him.

Give him a quick pat on the head and get on with your business for a few minutes. You can also help him relax by playing soft music in the background, leaving the television on low, or giving him a piece of clothing with your scent on it. Rottweilers with serious cases of separation anxiety may need anti-anxiety medication from your veterinarian, and both owner and pet will need to learn behavior modification techniques from a qualified professional trainer.

Von Willebrand's Disease (VWD)

VWD is an inherited bleeding disorder similar to hemophilia, with carriers often not exhibiting any symptoms. VWD is usually diagnosed by blood screening only when a Rottweiler has experienced prolonged bleeding or hemorrhaging after a wound or minor surgery. Transfusions and clotting medications are used to control VWD.

Emergency Procedures

Heatstroke

As previously mentioned, Rottweilers are more prone to heatstroke than many other breeds. Their dark black coat absorbs the heat and the dense inner coat holds it in. Overweight Rotties are at high risk for a heatstroke after just moderate exertion on a warm day. All dogs need to acclimate to a hot climate before engaging in any form of exercise, and water must be provided before, during, and after any outing in a hot climate. And just to reiterate: *Never leave a Rottie in a locked car on a sunny day, even if the outside temperature is mild.* Heatstroke can happen in 70°F (21°C) weather if the dog is forced to sit without shade, and is more likely when the dog is confined in a car.

Signs of heatstroke include rapid panting, bright red tongue and gums, thick saliva, vomiting, staggering or unsteadiness, and a temperature above 104°F (40°C). If your Rottie is exhibiting any of these signs, immediately start cooling measures. If outside, gently hose him off with cool—but not cold—water until he is strong enough to be taken inside. Place wet towels against his neck and abdomen, and between the legs. Concentrate on the neck and groin areas, as this is where the major arteries are found. If he is conscious, let him drink as much as he wants. If he is unconscious, do not try to force water into his mouth. *Seek immediate veterinary help*, as your Rottie may need some intravenous fluids and oxygen. Never apply alcohol on the pads or use ice packs, as they can actually burn the skin without cooling the dog's core.

Injuries

Speed is the most important factor when you

are dealing with an emergency situation. Should your Rottie sustain a serious injury, your first act must be to calm and restrain the dog so that he cannot move about and cause further damage to himself. Only then can you transport him to a veterinarian. Internal problems may be present that are not visible to the eye.

An injured dog is terrified and instinctively may lash out at anyone—even a beloved owner—who comes near him, so approach him cautiously. Speak in low, soothing tones. If you do not have a muzzle, try to devise an emergency muzzle (see TIP). You should never use a muzzle on a Rottie with chest injuries or if he is having difficulty breathing, however.

Move an injured animal only when absolutely necessary. Inspect the skin and locate the source of any bleeding. If possible, gently wash the area with soap and warm water. If the blood continues to flow, apply a clean cloth or gauze pad to the site, secure it if possible, and hold the compress in place until the bleeding stops. Unless the cut is very small, it will need professional attention. A veterinarian will be better able to apply a bandage that will stay in place.

If a bone appears to be broken, immobilize your Rottie to the best of your ability and get him to your veterinarian as quickly as possible. If allowed to move about, he may damage the muscles, tendons, cartilage, and nerves surrounding the break. Try to keep him calm. If necessary, you can use a blanket as a makeshift stretcher for transporting him short distances.

An injured dog can quickly go into shock, so cover him with a blanket for added warmth, and monitor his heart rate. Never give an injured dog anything to eat or drink. Knowing the dog's vital signs will be an aid for the veterinarian once help arrives. If the dog lapses into unconsciousness, check that his breathing passages are open. Get the dog onto his side. Gently pry open his mouth and pull the tongue forward to allow air to flow into the lungs.

Poisonings

Unfortunately, most accidental poisonings occur without the owner ever knowing that the dog has ingested a poisonous substance. This often has serious consequences, because *immediate* action is required if your Rottweiler is to survive a poisoning. Symptoms of poisoning include diarrhea, vomiting, lethargy, muscle spasms, shaking, dizziness, and increased salivation.

If you suspect that your Rottie has been poisoned, immediately seek professional help. Do not begin treating the dog yourself. The national poison control center, at (800) 222-1222 often can supply you with some advice, but your veterinarian should see the dog as quickly as possible.

If you know the cause of the poisoning, and have the packaging, some information on the proper antidote may be supplied on the container. It will aid your veterinarian greatly to know how much poison was ingested, and when, in order to formulate the proper method for getting it out of the dog's system. Various procedures are used, depending on what type of poison has been ingested. Sometimes the stomach is pumped; sometimes the poison is neutralized.

Many well-meaning owners have been the cause of poisonings by administering excessive amounts of over-the-counter worming products and flea and tick preparations. Because household items are the most common sources of poisoning (not only for house pets but also for children), owners must keep all cleaning agents, pesticides, medicines, and painting supplies locked up. Items stored in a garage or shed should be kept at a height that the dog cannot reach and must be secured carefully to avoid spills. Antifreeze is particularly dangerous for dogs. It has a pleasant odor and taste that may attract your Rottie to it, but the ingestion of even a tiny amount can cause severe kidney damage.

Never allow your Rottweiler to chew on plants, because many plants found in the house and garden are poisonous if ingested.

Your Aging Rottweiler

The life span of the average Rottweiler has increased a little over the last few decades from nine years to ten. This is attributed to better nutrition and better health care. Aside from having good genes, one major trait most geriatric Rotties have in common is that they have been lean throughout their life. Because of this, it is not as rare to see some happy and healthy 13- and even 14-year-old Rotties. These canine

senior citizens require some special care and may have some special limitations.

Daily Care

Let your older dog set his own pace. He will probably be stressed and resistant to change, so try to keep his daily routine intact as much as possible. Feed and walk him around the same time each day.

Rottweilers mature slowly and enjoy their peak physical condition from age three to six. The first sign of aging may be some gray hairs around the muzzle, followed by a slow loss of muscle tone. Coordination begins to wane around age seven, making walking across and getting up from bare floors difficult. If your house has wood or tile floors, consider placing some area rugs wherever your Rottie usually goes.

An elderly Rottweiler is also more sensitive to temperature changes. Heatstroke can come on quickly, so keep a close watch on him when out in hot weather and be extra careful when he is in the car. Be sure he is drinking, as dehydration can come on quickly and be life-threatening.

Drinking increased amounts of water may also be a sign of a health problem, so let

your veterinarian know of any significant change.

Your Rottweiler's sense of smell, hearing, and sight will decline with age. This may make his interest in food less acute, and he may seem less responsive to your commands when he actually doesn't hear them as well. Eye problems are particularly common, including cataracts, night blindness, and infections. Let your veterinarian know if your Rottie begins bumping into things or if there is any unusual discharge from his eyes.

Diet

As a dog ages, his digestive system may begin to give him problems. Any sudden weight change can indicate serious health problems. Weight loss has been associated with a degeneration of the ability of the liver and kidneys to properly manage waste. Weight gain may just be the result of a decrease in activity, but it can also be caused by an underlying disease, so be sure to weigh your dog regularly and feel his ribs for any sign of change.

One simple change that your elderly dog may appreciate is being given elevated food and water bowls, so he doesn't have to bend as much to eat or drink.

Constipation becomes more common in geriatric dogs (often because of prostate problems in males), but simple changes in his diet (such as adding a tablespoon of oat bran or canned pumpkin) can often help alleviate this. There are several high-quality diets on the market designed especially for older dogs or your veterinarian may suggest a "prescription" diet, which may have reduced levels of phosphorous and protein.

A once hearty eater that no longer finishes his bowl may do well to be given several small meals each day.

Arthritis

Even if your Rottweiler has been spared the problem of hip dysplasia throughout his life, he may still develop joint stiffness as he ages. Arthritis is common for many geriatric Rotties and will be aggravated if he is overweight or if he has been very physically active throughout his life. Climbing stairs and any sudden turns or jumps in an afflicted Rottie will become painful.

Arthritis and degenerative joint disease most often affects the hips, elbows, knees, and toes.

Symptoms may include swelling, lameness, a decrease in his range of motion, muscle wasting, and, above all, pain. Treatment includes painkillers and steroidal and nonsteroidal medications to reduce inflammation and slow the progression of the disease.

Incontinence

Urinary incontinence often develops as your Rottweiler ages, with sudden "accidents" or urinating in inappropriate places. This can be caused by bladder problems or inflammation and/or infection in the urinary tract or elsewhere. Your veterinarian will probably collect a urine sample to look for a bacterial infection and run additional blood tests to determine whether kidney damage is the cause. Many times incontinence can be controlled with medication. However, if your Rottie is showing signs of senility, he may not be aware that he is leaking urine.

Dental Problems

Dental problems and bad breath in elderly dogs often stem from excess tartar (plaque) buildup. This may make the teeth sensitive, which in turn may make your Rottie reluctant to eat.

Dogs with heavy plaque can develop systemwide health problems from bacteria entering the system through the problem teeth and inflamed gums. Many pet owners often regard dental care as a low priority, but the consequences of poor dental hygiene can be devas-

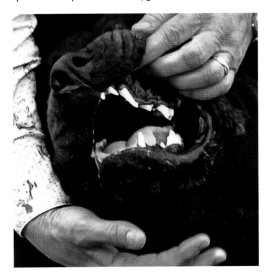

tating in the elderly Rottie. Your veterinarian may prescribe antibiotics before performing dental work, to avoid possible bacterial spread to the heart or other organs.

Calluses

As your Rottweiler ages, he will most likely develop thick calluses around his elbows. This builds up over years of hard contact with floors while getting up or lying down. Sleeping on tile or concrete can aggravate the condition. In severe cases an elbow hygroma—a fluid-filled sac—may form, which can be quite painful and may need to be drained. A heating pad will often help, and the dog may like lying on it. (Be sure to monitor all uses of a heating pad, as chewing could be deadly.)

There are a number of ointments that can help soften calluses, but your Rottie will usually lick it off before it gets a chance to work. You can increase your chances by applying the medicine, working it into the skin, and then immediately taking your Rottie for a walk or providing him with a better distraction than licking, such as a chew treat.

Providing your Rottie with thick, comfortable bedding placed where he likes to sleep will help in minimizing calluses.

Adipose Tumors

As your Rottweiler ages, he may develop benign tumors known as *adipose tumors* or *lipomas* (in laymen's terms: fat clumps). They are found in the subcutaneous layer of tissue directly under the skin and are slow growing. They are more common in bitches than males, and little is known about their cause.

Your veterinarian should investigate all such growths. Your veterinarian may do a quick nee-

dle biopsy to determine that they are, indeed, made of fat. If they grow large, they may have to be surgically removed, as they can press against any adjacent organ, but this is rare.

Senile Dementia

Senile dementia, also known as *canine cognitive dysfunction syndrome*, is similar to Alzheimer's disease in humans. Symptoms in elderly Rottweilers include disorientation with normal tasks, restlessness and an increased need for his owner's companionship, loss of bladder and bowel control, and decreased interest in or ability to interact with familiar humans or other pets.

There is no known cure, although some medications can slow the disease progression and its inherent decay of brain and body function. An afflicted Rottie will benefit from lots of attention and physical contact. He will sleep more and more, and it is important to provide him with comfortable bedding and additional warmth.

HOW-TO: MEDICAL CARE

A knowledgeable Rottweiler owner must be able to perform several simple procedures at home that will aid in assessing a pet's condition. Knowing how to take your pet's temperature and heart rate is vital when you suspect that your Rottie may be ill. By speedily performing these procedures you obtain some vital information about the animal's health—information that will be valuable for the veterinarian should the condition require emergency attention.

Taking the Temperature

Like humans, a dog often will respond to infection by running a fever. A dog's normal temperature is slightly higher than a human's—100.8°F to 102.5°F (38.2°–39.2°C). If you are lucky enough to own a state-of-the-art pet ear thermometer (approximately $50), it will take but a few seconds to get your Rottweiler's temperature. Taking a dog's temperature rectally, it is best to make it a two-person task. Lubricate the end of a heavy-duty rectal thermometer—regular or digital—with a little petroleum or KY jelly. One person calms and restrains the Rottie while the other lifts the tail, inserts the thermometer about 1 inch (2.5 cm), and pre-

vents him from sitting down. The thermometer should remain for one to two minutes for a mercury thermometer to get an accurate reading or until the digital beeps.

Any reading below 99°F (37.2°C) or above 104°F (40°C) is considered extremely serious and your Rottie should be taken to a veterinarian immediately.

Taking the Pulse

A dog's heartbeat and pulse also can be monitored easily. A Rottweiler's heart normally beats from 60 to 100 times per minute while resting, but this rate may vary because of such factors as age, physical condition, external temperature, exertion, stress, and illness. To feel the heartbeat, you can place your fingertips against your dog's chest just behind his elbow, but this is less precise than taking a pulse rate. A pulse can be found in the front paw, but the one on the inside of the thigh near the groin is the easiest to locate. Press softly against the artery there to find the pulse and monitor the pattern and rate of the beats. This procedure should be performed if you ever notice signs of extreme fatigue, fainting, or hyperac-

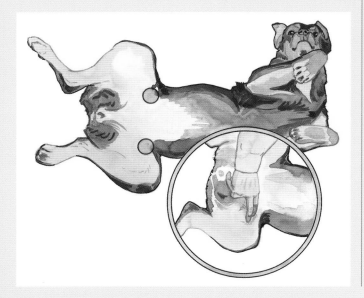

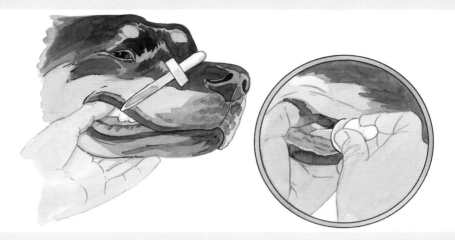

tivity in your dog. Any abnormal patterns in the heartbeat require immediate attention by a veterinarian.

You also should be aware of your dog's normal breathing pattern. When relaxed, the breathing should be easy and smooth, from 10 to 30 breaths per minute.

Giving Medication

Giving your Rottweiler a pill or capsule may seem like a simple enough procedure, but most Rotties quickly master the technique for not swallowing pills and defiantly spitting them right back out. The easiest method is to disguise the pill in something tasty, such as a small chunk of liverwurst, hamburger meat, or a piece of cheese that is swallowed quickly in one gulp. If your Rottie is not so easily tricked, gently pry his mouth open by applying pressure at the back of his mouth, tilt his head up slightly, and insert the pill as far back on the tongue as possible. Close his jaws, give him a distracting pat, and watch for a swallow. Gently stroking the

throat may encourage a reluctant dog to swallow. *Never lift his head straight up and drop in a pill, as in this position the medicine can be inhaled into the windpipe rather than swallowed.*

The best way to administer liquid medicine is to place it in a medicine spoon or syringe and pour it into the *back of his mouth* by lifting up the side of his lower lip by the back molars and holding the head *slightly* upward. This allows the medicine to slide down the throat. Keep a grasp around his muzzle until you are sure he has swallowed, or he may spit the medicine out. Again, never hold his head in an exaggerated upward position, as this invites choking.

Some liquid and powdered medicines also may be mixed into your Rottie's food (check with your veterinarian first, however), but many can smell or taste the additives right away and will not eat the "tainted" food. If this is the case, powdered medications usually can be liquefied by adding a little water, and you can proceed as described above.

INFORMATION

Rottweiler Breed Clubs

The American Rottweiler Club
www.amrottclub.org

Doris Baldwin, Public Information/
    Breeder Referral
P.O. Box 23741
Pleasant Hill, CA 94523

Gwen Chaney, President/Breed Rescue
5014 Granger Street
Indianapolis, IN 46268
E-mail: ejchaneyjr@aol.com

Judge's Education
Cathleen Rubens
971 Luther Road
Apex, NC 27523

Rottweiler Club of Canada
E-mail: secretary@rottclub.ca
33-2825 Gananoque Drive
Mississauga, ON L5N 1V6 Canada

International Kennel Clubs

American Kennel Club
260 Madison Avenue
New York, NY 10016
www.akc.org

United Kennel Club
100 East Kilgore Road
Kalamazoo, MI 49002
www.ukcdogs.com

Canadian Kennel Club
200 Ronson Drive, Suite 400
Etobicoke, ON M9W 5Z9 Canada
www.ckc.ca

The Kennel Club
1-5 Clarges Street, Piccadilly
London W1J 8AB England
www.the-kennel-club.org.uk

Australian National Kennel Council
Royal Show Grounds
Ascot Vale
Victoria, Australia
www.ankc.org.au

Irish Kennel Club
Fottrell House
Harolds X Bridge
Dublin 6W Ireland
www.ikc.ie

New Zealand Kennel Club
Prosser Street
Private Bag 50903
Porirua 5240 New Zealand
www.nzkc.org.nz

Organizations

AKC Canine Health Foundation
P.O. Box 37941
Raleigh, NC 27627

American Society for the Prevention
    of Cruelty to Animals
424 East 92nd Street
New York, NY 10128
www.aspca.org

American Veterinary Medical Association
1931 North Meacham Road, Suite 100
Schaumberg, IL 60173
www.avma.org

Canine Eye Registration Foundation
1717 Philo Road
P.O. Box 3007
Urbana, IL 61803
www.vmdb.org/cerf.html

Canine Health Information Center
2300 E. Nifong Boulevard
Columbia, MO 65201
www.caninehealthinfo.org

The Delta Society
875 124th Avenue NE, Suite 101
Bellevue, WA 98005
www.deltasociety.org

Humane Society of the United States
2100 L Street, NW
Washington, DC 20037
www.hsus.org

National Dog Registry
P.O. Box 51105
Mesa, AZ 85208
www.nationaldogregistry.com

Orthopedic Foundation for Animals
2300 E. Nifong Boulevard
Columbia, MO 65201
www.offa.org

Pet Care Services Association
(formerly, American Boarding Kennel Association)
1702 East Pikes Peak Avenue
Colorado Springs, CO 80909
www.petcareservices.org

Pet Sitters International
201 East King Street
King, NC 27021
www.petsit.com

The Seeing Eye
P.O. Box 375
Morristown, NJ 07963
www.seeingeye.org

Therapy Dogs International
88 Bartley Road
Flanders, NJ 07836
www.tdi-dog.org/

Books

In addition to the most recent edition of the official publication of the AKC, *The Complete Dog Book*, published by Howell Book House, in New York, there are the following:

Alderton, David. *The Dog Care Manual.* Hauppauge, NY: Barron's Educational Series, Inc., 1986.
Baer, Ted. *Communicating with Your Dog.* Hauppauge, NY: Barron's Educational Series, Inc., 1989.
Frye, Fredric. *First Aid for Your Dog.* Hauppauge, NY: Barron's Educational Series, Inc., 1987.
Klever, Ulrich. *The Complete Book of Dog Care.* Hauppauge, NY: Barron's Educational Series, Inc., 1989.
Ullmann, Hans-J. *The New Dog Handbook.* Hauppauge, NY: Barron's Educational Series, Inc., 1985.

About the Author

Kerry Kern, formerly Managing Editor of the *Canine Graphic,* has written extensively on the subject of dogs. She is the author of *Labrador Retrievers, Siberian Huskies,* and *The New Terrier Handbook* (Barron's).

A Note on Pronouns

Many dog lovers feel that the pronoun "it" is not appropriate when referring to a beloved pet. For this reason, Rottweilers are described as "Festus," "Rottie," or "he" throughout this book unless the topic specifically relates to female dogs. This by no means infers any preference, nor should it be taken as an indication that either sex is particularly problematic.

Important Note

This book is concerned with buying, keeping, and raising Rottweilers. The publisher and the author think it is important to point out that the advice and information for Rottweiler maintenance applies to healthy, normally developed and socialized animals. Anyone who buys an adult Rottweiler or adopts one from an animal shelter must consider that the animal may have behavioral problems and may, for example, bite without any visible provocation. Such anxiety–biters are dangerous for the owner as well as for the general public. Be sure to consult with an experienced trainer when bringing an adult Rottweiler into the home.

Caution is further advised in the association of children with a Rottweiler, in meetings with other dogs, and in exercising the dog without a leash.

Cover Photos

Front cover: Shutterstock; back cover: Cheryl A. Ertelt; inside front cover: Kent Akselsen; inside back cover: Cheryl A. Ertelt.

Photo Credits

Kent Akselsen: pages 12, 44, 56, 57, 68, 80, 86; Tara Darling: pages 2–3, 8, 15, 18, 39, 47, 50, 71, 73, 83; Cheryl A. Ertelt: pages 4, 5, 17, 19, 21, 32, 33, 38, 41, 48, 51, 54, 58, 65, 66, 70; Shirley Fernandez/Paulette Johnson: page 74; Isabelle Francais: pages 6, 16, 22, 24, 27, 28, 30, 35, 40, 53, 72, 79, 82, 87, 89, 93, 95, 96, 100, 102; Paulette Johnson: pages 31, 78, 81, 98, 99; Zig Leszczynski: page 90; Pet Profiles: pages 11, 23, 104; Pets by Paulette: pages 13, 14, 42, 43, 60, 62, 63, 64, 75, 77, 85, 94; Shutterstock: pages 25, 55, 103, 105; Connie Summers/Paulette Johnson: pages 9, 20, 29, 69.

All inquiries should be addressed to:
Barron's Educational Series, Inc.
250 Wireless Boulevard
Hauppauge, NY 11788
www.barronseduc.com

ISBN-13: 978-0-7641-4225-3
ISBN-10: 0-7641-4225-9

Library of Congress Control Number: 2009927378

Printed in China
9 8 7 6 5 4 3 2 1